You Won't Start Winning Without a Beginning—
Learn How to Start Winning Today with This Uplifting Book.

"Hard-hitting and uplifting messages . . . The one I love most is: 'Turn your scars into stars!' Bob is doing it, I'm doing it, anybody can do it—if he believes and expects a miracle."
—Oral Roberts

"Terrific. I couldn't put it down."
—Rich de Vos, President,
Amway Corporation

"The best thing about Pastor Schuller's upbeat philosophy is that he does not just 'point' the way to self-improvement; he 'leads' us. His new book for our anxious generation is by a man who's been there—and back. He *is* 'tough people'; this book tells us how *we can be.*"
—Paul Harvey

"Without a doubt, Dr. Robert Schuller will go down in history as one of those people who helped to change the world by changing people's attitudes about themselves . . . By changing your attitude you can change your life, and he has done that with countless thousands."
—Mary Kay Ash

"Full of inspiring examples. Practical advice is sprinkled throughout the book, which is written in a sprightly, entertaining manner. It will be a treasured volume in my library."
—Jay Van Andel, Chairman,
Amway Corporation

Dr. Robert H. Schuller is one of the most widely known churchmen in America today. Every Sunday, more than 10,000 worshippers crowd into his Crystal Cathedral to hear his unique spiritual message, and millions more hear this message on his extraordinary television program, "The Hour of Power." Now in *Tough Times Never Last, But Tough People Do!* he brings a remarkable message to everyone, anywhere, who seeks a fresh start.

QUANTITY PURCHASES

TOUGH TIMES
Never Last,
But Tough
People Do!

ROBERT H. SCHULLER

BANTAM BOOKS
TORONTO · NEW YORK · LONDON · SYDNEY · AUCKLAND

TOUGH TIMES NEVER LAST, BUT TOUGH PEOPLE DO!

A Bantam Book / published by arrangement with
Thomas Nelson, Inc.

PRINTING HISTORY

Thomas Nelson edition published May 1983
An American Circle Book Club and Preferred Choice
Bookplan Selection
Serialized in National Enquirer.
8 printings through December 1983
Bantam edition / June 1984

Bantam Books are published by Bantam Books, Inc. Its trademark,
consisting of the words "Bantam Books" and the portrayal of a rooster,
is Registered in U.S. Patent and Trademark Office and in other
countries. Marca Registrada. Bantam Books, Inc., 666 Fifth Avenue,
New York, New York 10103.

PRINTED IN THE UNITED STATES OF AMERICA

H   0 9

To my grandchildren:
Angie Rae Schuller
Robert Vernon Schuller
Jason James Coleman
Christopher John Coleman

CONTENTS

Acknowledgments

This book would not have been possible without the help of Sheila Schuller Coleman who organized and edited the manuscript. I also want to thank Barbara Hagler for typing the manuscript and Marjorie Kelley for her careful assistance.

PREFACE

Lord,
give me the guidance
to know
when to hold on
and
when to let go
and the grace
to make the right decision
with dignity.

This could be the most important prayer you've ever prayed, and this book could be the answer to that prayer. For this book will provoke you to tough action: (a) To hold on until the light breaks, the tide turns, and the times change for the better; to tenaciously dig in and bloom where you are planted; to inspire people with your cheerful attitude while you are going through such obviously difficult times. In the process you will inspire others to choose the noble and positive outlook.

Or (b) this book will inspire you to take action to make a bold and daring move; to make a creative transition, recognizing an era has come to an end. The factory will never reopen. The steam engines are never going to be manufactured again. Sometimes the cup has fallen. It is broken. "All the king's horses and all the king's men couldn't put Humpty Dumpty together again." Now you may need to absorb the spills and develop new skills. This book will get you started on the path to success once again.

PART I

Tough Times Never Last, But Tough People Do!

1

Tough Times Never Last . . .

It was a harsh summer, the summer of '82. For many, it was as if the clocks had rolled back to the thirties and the time of the Great Depression. Company upon company declared bankruptcy. Unemployment soared. The "severe and prolonged recession," as it was dubbed by the media, sent ripples of depression across America.

Politicians used the depressed state of the country to their advantage. It provided a great opportunity to highlight the failures, shortcomings, and faults of the opposite political party. Democrats found in it an opportunity to blame the Republican administration which was in charge. Predictably, the Republicans, in turn, blamed the "Democratic administration that created the problem" which the Republicans had inherited.

Everybody was fixing the blame—nobody was fixing the problem!

The problems persisted. They grew. The recession ran rampant across the country until nearly everyone was affected by it. No one was immune.

I, personally, felt it as pastor of the Crystal Cathedral congregation and head of a national television ministry, which was broadcast on 169 television stations every week. With five hundred people on the payroll, we were operating on a budget of well over twenty million dollars a year. The cost of operations continued to increase dramatically. Like the rest of America, we too were faced with tough economic times.

No one could deny that the country had problems. But the biggest problem we had was our *attitude* toward the economic problem. Negative thinking spread like a plague through all levels of society. It was not easy to protect oneself from the infection of negative thinking, which spread by word of mouth, by conversations with friends as well as strangers, by television screens, and by radio news reports.

It spread quickly because in recessive times the tendency is to react negatively. Once an organism, a business, a life, or a country is infected with negative thinking, the infection attacks the mind, the heart, and the soul like termites that secretly gnaw away at the emotional support system.

It was in the midst of this national mood that I arrived at the Hilton Hotel in downtown Chicago. I was there to present a motivational lecture at a major convention.

Delivering lectures of inspiration as well as on successful management principles was nothing new to me. Each year I travel from coast to coast, giving nearly one hundred talks to doctors, executives, educators, you name it.

However, I was particularly fascinated by this engagement. My audience would be members of the Ag-Industry. ("Ag" is, of course, the abbreviation for *agriculture*.) This industry represents those who are involved in the farming enterprises of the Midwest states of Iowa, Michigan, Illinois, and Minnesota. Having been born and reared on an Iowa farm, I looked upon this as an opportunity to touch base with some of the people that came from the same soil I left forty years before.

My anticipation of a warm, inspirational evening was quickly doused by a couple of somber-looking gentlemen. The convention badges pinned to their dark lapels identified them as the men for whom I was looking. They greeted me with restrained enthusiasm. "Dr. Schuller? Thank you for coming."

Their words reminded me of the thousands of times I have arrived at some scene of tragedy. In hospitals, mortuaries, courtrooms, and cemeteries, I have heard those words: "Thank you for coming." I couldn't help feeling that I had arrived at the scene of some tragedy, rather than at a motivational convention.

The younger man spoke: "There are thirty-five hundred people in there waiting to hear you speak."

His companion interrupted. "These people are going through tough times. They don't want to hear your funny stories. They don't want to see you grinning from ear to ear like you do on television. They don't want a pat on the back with a hollow promise that 'Everything is going to be okay.'"

At that point, both men moved shoulder to shoulder to face me as if they meant to block me from entering the platform. The first man spoke up, "That's right, Dr. Schuller. These people are losing their farms. Their businesses are going bankrupt. Terrible pressures are being placed on their marriages and families. They need help. And more than anything else they need hope. Give it to them."

With that admonishment they nodded to the sound man, who pinned the microphone to my suit. As he did, I heard through the thin wall that separated the backstage area from the speaker's platform, the master of ceremonies' introduction: "Ladies and gentlemen, it is my pleasure now to introduce our keynote speaker. His name is Dr. Robert Schuller. He is the pastor of the world-famous Crystal Cathedral. This beautiful building was built at a cost of over twenty million dollars and was dedicated virtually debt-free. No minister or priest or rabbi speaks to more people every week in the world or in the United States of America than does Dr. Robert Schuller from Garden Grove, California. It's our pleasure now to welcome one of the world's most successful men—Dr. Robert Schuller. Let's give him a great welcome!"

The sound of enthusiastic applause surrounded me as I stepped onstage to face this collection of depressed souls. Thirty-five hundred people were on their feet, applauding me. The grand ballroom was packed to capacity.

Inwardly I shuddered. My carefully planned speech had just gone out the window. The three jokes I was prepared to tell for my own pleasure and for the purpose of "warming up my audience" now seemed out of place.

I found myself walking across the stage without the faintest idea of what I would tell these troubled people. I paced quietly from one end of the platform to the other, trying to collect my thoughts. I searched the eyes of the audience. I recalled the words of the stern welcoming committee. I decided to recover my position by asking a question.

"They tell me that you are having tough times. Is that right?"

The question gave me time to embrace a dramatic pause. Such a pause can be a lifesaver to a public speaker.

I continued to pace back and forth, pretending to exude the confidence of a well-prepared lecturer.

I could tell that my opening question had grabbed their attention—probably more effectively than the three funny stories I had carefully placed in my front pocket.

From that point on I delivered a spontaneous lecture that at times erupted with new insights. Wanting desperately to help these people and give them hope, I decided to address myself specifically to the pressing problems of these men and women who represented an industry vital to the health and welfare of our country. They represented the core of the breadbasket of America. The food in the markets and on the tables of our country comes from the labor and the leadership of these agriculture businessmen and women.

I remembered years ago what I was taught in my undergraduate studies in public speaking, lecturing, debating, and oratorical work in Hope College, Holland, Michigan, and again in my training at Western Theological Seminary in preparation for delivering sermons and talks from pulpits: the most effective speech is not a sermon but a witness. Essentially the principle is this: If you don't have any advice to give, you can always share your own story.

If there has been any excitement, challenge, crisis, and resolution in your life, then share it! Everybody likes a good story.

Drawing on this principle, I decided to share with the farmers how I handled the tough times in my life.

I suspected that my audience was not aware of the fact that

I, too, had tough times. My introduction portrayed me only as a very successful man, senior minister, founder and builder of a twenty-million-dollar, internationally acclaimed work of art called the Crystal Cathedral. They could only perceive me as very successful. They had not been told that I, too, had walked a path similar to the one they were now walking.

Should I tell them about the time a twenty-below-zero blizzard raged through the lonely blackness of an Iowa night?

Should I tell them how the wind whistled around the fragile country house, successfully penetrating the cracks between the window frame in the northwest corner of my bedroom, leaving fresh drifts of snow on the floor beside my bed?

Should I tell them how we didn't have the money to buy coal to warm the house?

Should I tell them how we raced to escape with our lives from a tornado?

Should I tell them how we survived the great drought, when the shortage of natural rainfall parched the earth and proved more devastating and destructive than the shortage of cash flow that had already hit all of the Americans in the Great Depression?

Should I tell them about my struggles to get through college?

Should I tell them about the fire in my rooming house in which I lost the few possessions I had?

Should I tell them how I had to struggle to start a church with only five hundred dollars, in a strange state without friends, contacts, property, or community support?

Should I tell them about my wife's bout with cancer? The near-loss of my daughter's life in a motorcycle accident? The amputation of her leg?

Should I share with them our struggles of the past three years, as we have tried to help her accommodate effectively to life as a young teen-ager with a disfigured, left stump of a leg?

~ Should I tell them how I was forced by circumstances beyond my control to build the Crystal Cathedral when I didn't want to build it, didn't have the money, and knew well enough that I would be criticized for building a "monument"?

I decided not to pour out my whole life story. But I did decide to begin with the realities of the tough times I had been through and how they had been handled successfully through a faith based on possibility thinking.

"Farming life has never been easy. My boyhood farm was a typical Midwestern farm. That meant it was small. The industry was not simple crop farming. The crops were harvested and fed to livestock. Chickens laid the eggs, which we traded for groceries. Cows grazed the grassland along the river that was too difficult to plow. We milked the cows and sold the milk. When the hogs reached their prime weight, they were sold at market. It was a one-crop-a-year farm. That meant that we planted the oats and the corn in the springtime and harvested it in the fall, to be gathered into barns and saved for feed for the hogs. The winter season was merely a time of survival—waiting and hoping for spring."

My father purchased our farm when prices were at their peak. Real estate had been climbing steadily. I was born only a few years later, September 16, 1926.

How my father saved enough to buy our farm is a story in itself. Because he lost his parents as a teen-ager, Dad was forced to drop out of school in the sixth grade and to find the only job he could—as a hired hand for the local farmers. One could always husk corn: Rip each single golden ear from its nest of leaves, crack off the six-foot stem, and throw it into the wagon. My father was a thrifty young man and was able to save a few nickels and dimes that he earned for each ear of corn he picked.

Finally he had saved enough to purchase a 160-acre farm. Unfortunately he bought it at the top of the price cycle. When I was three years old the Great Depression hit. Real estate prices plummeted along with the stocks. While internationally famed corporate chiefs were committing suicide in Wall Street, lonely farmers—America's original small businessmen—were clinging with broken fingernails to the earth, hoping to survive.

My father was one of those tough, tenacious farmers. Winter was the worst. I shall never forget the times when we did not have money to buy coal. The trees that surrounded the house were considered precious living creatures that could not be sacrificed for fuel. So we never considered cutting them down and sawing them up for the wood-burning stove.

Instead it became my job, as a child, to step over the three-foot high splintered wooden fence and climb into the hog yard among the one hundred squirming, squealing hogs. With an empty basket I maneuvered my way through the excrement, picking up every corncob left after the hogs had consumed the kernels.

Not a single cob was left uncollected. Every single one was considered of real value. When the basket was filled, I would carefully carry it to the tiny two-story, white sideboard home where my mother, father, brother, and sisters lived. The corncobs would fuel the stove in the kitchen. They would also be used in the potbelly stove in the little living room. These were the only two sources of heat in the house. Little grills in the ceilings allowed some of the heat to pass from the downstairs kitchen and living room to the upstairs bedrooms. But cracks in the walls let in just as much freezing air.

"Do you want to hear about my experience with poverty?" I said to the struggling thirty five hundred businessmen, seated in the carpeted ballroom of the plush Hilton Hotel. "Let me tell you about poverty. I was so poor we had to use corncobs to heat our homes to keep from freezing to death in the subzero winters. We used corncobs because we could not afford coal."

"Those were tough times!" I bellowed.

Then I recalled the years of the great drought. Even as the economic depression ravaged the country, the Iowa farmers fought a far tougher battle. For reasons we never understood, the normal spring rainfall never came to moisten the newly planted corn and oats. The few precious dollars that my father was able to save had to be spent on seed corn.

I always wondered how he dared to risk throwing seed in the ground where it might rot and die, when he could safely bring it to town and convert it to cash. "Why take a chance?" I once asked my father. "Why don't you play it safe and sell it?"

"People who never take a chance," he taught me wisely, "never get ahead."

Of course, there is no success without the application of the multiplication principle. It was a natural, native, basic principle that every farmer understood. So in the springs of 1931, 1932, and 1933 my father took all that he had left—the last kernels of corn, the last cups of oats—and planted them in the ground of his small Iowa farm, expecting that the rains would fall. He hoped that the seeds would become wet and bloated until they erupted with new life, sending their tender little sprouts up through the softened spring soil. Light-green rows of corn would begin to grow and stand out against the black background of the dark Iowa ground.

Rainfall is essential to a farmer's success. And Iowa farmers can expect rain to fall at least once every other week.

If, for some reason, the rains did not fall for three or four weeks, one inch of the topsoil would dry out first. Then, if rain still did not come, the soil would gradually grow dry at two, three, four, five inches deep, until the hair-like tentacles of the roots of the new corn plants would die.

The first evidence of the death of the roots would be a wilted leaf.

When the rains did not fall for two weeks, my father was worried. When the third and fourth weeks passed with no rain I saw his face grow very grave. Not once did he become angry. Never did he miss praying with bowed head at the table before our morning, noon, or nighttime meals.

The only thing my father did about the drought was pray. That was the only thing he could do. Farmers gathered from miles around, at special prayer meetings, filling the little white churches that dotted the rolling landscapes. Out of respect and reverence to the almighty God, each farmer came, not in his overalls, but in his one and only suit and tie.

They called upon God Almighty to save their land and their crops. They asked Him to send rain.

Then all they could do was to go home and wait for His answer. For a whole year the Lord was silent. Day after day, the sun bore down on the crops. Every day we thirstily scanned the scorching sky for a sign of a cloud. More than once I ran into the house, calling out, "I've seen a cloud! God may be answering our prayer!" But the clouds always dissipated.

Finally, as if in fact our prayers were being answered, there was a gathering of clouds. Hopes began to rise again. The desperately needed rainfall was moving in from the west! Flashes of lightning slashed through the black sky. Thunder cracked. The trees trembled with fright as the wind whipped through their branches. It rained!

I was jubilant, but my father did not share my enthusiasm. Neither did my mother. For they knew what I did not know: the rain was totally inadequate. When the last thunder clap echoed in the distance, signaling the passing of the storm, the sun came out bright and hot again. We walked outdoors. My father scooped up a handful of the wet, moistened surface soil. Only the top quarter-inch was wet and black. Below that the earth was powdery dry.

Then the winds began to blow—from where we did not know. The sky turned from bright blue to a drab gray to a dirty brown. And the clean bright air that I enjoyed breathing as a child suddenly became polluted with dust. "That's South Dakota land you are breathing, Son," my father said. South Dakota, the state that bordered Iowa on the northwest, was suffering a worse drought than Iowa. It did not even enjoy the sporadic showers that moistened the surface soil. The barren land, devoid of any vegetation, lay helpless before the gathering winds. They swept the feathery particles of earth high into the sky, carrying them hundreds of miles to the east. Like drifts of snow the dust settled on our farm. When the winds blew harder, the dust sandblasted the few rows of corn that had managed to survive the drought. The fragile young plants, wilted and weakened for want of refreshing

Nobody is a
total failure
if he dares
to try
to do something
worthwhile.

water, were no match for the grit driven by the hot winds. There was total devastation. Here and there, like bones of a dead animal, dead corn stalks protruded above the drift of dry sand.

Still the winds did not cease. It became a common procedure for my brother, sisters, and me to cover our faces with wet cloths as we walked the short distance from our house to the outdoor toilet. When we walked to the well, where we hoped we would be able to pump water from the forty-foot reservoir, we would have to protect ourselves from the suffocating dust with our moistened masks.

Our water became more and more scarce as the meandering snake of a river dried up. The Floyd River had been my closest childhood friend. On its green banks, near open pastures, I would lie, watching the clouds change shape in the blue sky. It was there that I felt closest to my Creator.

I became incurably addicted to God's natural green gardens. Years later, I would hope and dream of a place where I could worship and see the sky above me, day and night. Years later I would dream of a church that could allow all of the sky to permeate our troubled minds with its peace, bringing healing from worry and anxiety. Years later I would find that dream fulfilled in a Crystal Cathedral.

But during the summer of the great drought, I watched the river dry up. Little pools of water became mud holes where squirming bullhead catfish died. We were surrounded by death—the river was dead, the fish were dead, and most importantly, the crops were dead.

Summer finally gave way to fall. Newspapers nationwide proclaimed the Midwest farm belt to be in "total disaster." Even the New York bankers and corporate chiefs became concerned about a plague that was as great, if not greater, than their own economic depression. The breadbasket of America was in ruins.

If it had been a normal year, my father would have expected to harvest corn that would fill dozens of wagons. That year, my father harvested barely a half a wagon of corn, grown on a half-acre of ground. In a normal year, this swampy lot, fed by some mysterious underground spring, was too wet to produce any fruit at all.

My father had often thought about digging deep into that plot to drain the subsurface water away. Now in the year of the drought this small plot of ground was the only parcel out of 160 acres where the corn had survived. Here the corn lived, drawing moisture from a subterranean source. Here the corn grew nearly six feet tall. And here we harvested the minuscule crop.

It was but half a wagon of corn.

A total disaster? Not quite. For a half a wagon of corn was better than none at all. In fact, it was equal to the amount of seed that had been sowed earlier that year. A total loss? No. We gained nothing. But more importantly we lost nothing!

I shall never forget my father's dinnertime prayer that night.

"Dear Lord. I thank You that I have lost nothing this year. You have given me my seed back. Thank You!"

Not all farmers had as much faith as my father did.

"For sale" signs began to appear on farm after farm. Discouraged farmers who could not imagine that things would get better packed up and abandoned their land. Other farmers simply threw their hands up in despair and allowed the bank to foreclose. More than one piece of property sold on the courthouse steps.

Years later I asked my father how he had survived. After all, he had had no cash reserves. He had had no rich relatives.

"I went to the bank," my father said, "and I promised them that if they would help me, somehow I'd return their money. I pleaded with them to refinance, rearrange the mortgage, postpone the due date. For some reason, the bank believed in me and it helped."

I remember that bank! I have early childhood memories of going there, in patched overalls, with my father. I recall seeing this slogan on a calendar in that bank: *"Great people are ordinary people with extraordinary amounts of determination."*

I'm convinced that that slogan exemplified the positive attitude of my father and inspired the bankers to go along with him and give him an extension on his mortgage payment.

That slogan was an explanation of my father's success and an inspiration to me to attempt the impossible too! For I had dreams of my own—to go to college and seminary.

Some years later, on a quiet June afternoon, the tornado struck. I had not unpacked my suitcases, having returned only a few days before for the summer recess from my college studies. Throughout the afternoon, my dad and I could hear an awesome roar reverberating like the hum of a mighty organ. The eerie sound was like many freight trains rumbling above the threatening and gathering clouds.

"Sounds like we're in for a hailstorm," my dad murmured.

In a desperate attempt to protect his prize roses, we rounded up empty pails and wooden boxes to cover every treasured bush. It was six o'clock now. We had finished our evening meal in haste. From the vantage point of our front lawn we could see more than a mile across the rolling farm land. The sun was lost now, seemingly swallowed by the black monstrous storm that was prowling the western sky.

Slowly, with alarming stillness like a tiger crawling up on a sleeping prey, the storm crept closer. Gusts of hot wind blew the dry dust of the country road. The old box elder bent before the mounting winds.

Out in the pasture a cow bellowed frantically, calling her little calf to come to her side for safety.

My riding horse seemed to sense impending disaster. He cut a commanding picture, standing erect, with head held high, graceful neck arched. His tail, lifted slightly, fanned in the wind; his ears searched the air for sounds of danger.

Suddenly a black lump, about the size of the sun, bulged out of the black sky. In an instant it telescoped to the ground in a long gray funnel. For a moment it hung suspended—like a slithering serpent, about to strike death to helpless victims below. Dad called to Mom: "It's a tornado, Jennie!"

I asked excitedly, "Are you sure it's a real tornado, Dad?" My first emotion was delightful excitement. This would be something to tell the fellows when I returned to Hope College in the fall. The funnel seemed so small I couldn't imagine the fury that could be unleashed from such a funny cloud.

"Call Mother, Son, and tell her to take whatever she can grab and come to the car. We've got to get out of here—right away!"

A moment later we were driving crazily down the road. We lived on the east end of a dead-end road and had to drive a mile west, directly into the path of the oncoming tornado in order to reach a side road that led south, away from the path of the storm. We made it.

Two miles south, we parked our car on the crest of the hill and watched the wicked twister spend its killing power. As quickly and quietly as it had dropped, it lifted and disappeared. It was all over. The storm was gone. The air was deathly still, but the danger was past. Gentle raindrops now began to fall. The tail end of the dark sky dropped a soothing shower of cool rain, as if heaven were pouring a soothing balm on fresh wounds.

We could go home now. "Oh, God, will we find our house?" We reached the crossroads, only to find a long line of cars. Curious sightseers, sensing that something terrible had happened, already were gathering. They were looking at the complete destruction of a neighboring farm.

Wondering if our house had been spared, we drove down the lonely road, crisscrossed by wires from broken telephone poles, toward our secluded farm. We came to the base of the hill that hid the view of our house. Before, we had been able to see the peak of our barn. But not now. We knew before we went over the hill that our barn was gone.

Now we were on the top of the hill. We saw it. Everything was gone. Where only a half hour before there had been nine buildings, freshly painted, now there were none. Where there had been life, there was the silence of death. It was all gone—all dead.

Only white foundations remained, lying on a clean patch of black ground. There was no debris. Everything had simply been sucked up and carried away. Three little pigs, still liv-

*When
you've exhausted
all possibilities,
remember this:
You haven't!*

ing, suckled the breasts of their dead mother, lying in the driveway. We could hear the sickening moan of dying cattle, the hiss of gas escaping from a portable tank of butane used to provide fuel for our stove. Then I saw my riding horse—lying dead with a fourteen-foot-long two-by-four piercing his belly.

Dazed, our brains reeling, we sat in our car. My father was past sixty and had worked hard for twenty-six years to try to win this farm. The mortgage was about due. This seemed to kill all chances of ever saving the place from the creditors. I looked at my dad, sitting horror-stricken, white-haired, underweight from overwork, his hands blue, desperately gripping the steering wheel.

Suddenly those calloused hands with their bulging blood vessels began hitting the steering wheel of the car, and Dad cried, "It's all gone! Jennie! Jennie, it's all gone! Twenty-six years, Jennie, and it's all gone in ten minutes."

Dad got out of the car, ordering us to wait, and walked with his cane around the clean-swept, tornado-vacuumed farmyard.

We later found out that our house had been dropped, in one smashed piece, a half-mile out in the pasture. We had had a little sign on the kitchen wall—a little molded plaster motto. Its simple verse was: "Keep looking to Jesus." My dad found and carried to the car the broken top half: "Keep looking. . . ." Well, this was God's message to Dad—Keep looking! Keep looking!

Don't quit now. Don't sell out. Dig in and hold on. And he did! People thought my dad was finished, but he was not. He was not finished because he would not give up. He had faith with hanging-on power! There's one ingredient that mountain-moving faith, miracle-generating faith, earth-shaking faith, problem-solving faith, and situation-changing faith must have, and that ingredient is *holding* power. So Dad didn't quit.

Two weeks later we found in a nearby town an old house that was being torn down. A section of it was available for sale for fifty dollars. So we bought this remnant and took it apart, piece by piece. We saved every nail and every shingle. And from these pieces we built a new little house on the old home farm! One by one, additional farm buildings were built. Nine farms were demolished in that tornado but my father was the only farmer to rebuild a completely demolished farm. A few years later prices rose sharply. Farm products prospered. Within five years the mortgage was paid off. My father died a successful man![1]

"So you're having tough times! Are they tougher times than my father experienced?" I looked deep into the eyes and the hearts of the new generation of Iowa farmers. "Are you burning corncobs for fuel? Have you lost everything in a tornado? Is the mortgage due and the cash not there? Are you tempted to walk away and put the place up for sale? Then let me tell you something about tough times. I believe I have walked the path and have earned the right to comment on tough times. Let me tell you something about tough times!"

I hadn't the foggiest idea *what* I was going to tell them about tough times! I had painted myself into a corner. I prayed silently. I prolonged the dramatic pause as I paced like a tiger in a cage back and forth across the empty stage, returning the stares of a very attentive audience.

I was stunned to hear this sentence come out of my mouth. I was shocked. I was inspired! I am convinced it came directly from God. It was a sentence that would not only inspire me and my audience but many others. It would even give birth to a book. Like a thunderclap, this sentence filled every corner of the huge ballroom:

Tough times never last, but tough people do!

The place broke up with applause. Those thirty-five hundred farmers who had lost hope and had battled depres-

---

[1]The tornado story is an excerpt from *Move Ahead With Possibility Thinking.* Copyright © 1967 by Robert H. Schuller. Reprinted by permission of Doubleday and Company, Inc.

sion found that hope. They caught a new vision and began to dream again.

Are you facing tough times today? Overwhelmed? I invite you to take a walk with me. Let me tell you about survivors—and how *you* can be one too! In the process your life will become a light for someone else's pathway.

The path is called "The Possibility Thinking Path." I've been preaching it for years. It has never let me down. It has never let anybody down. It never quits on us. We may quit the path, but the path keeps right on going on to happiness, health, and prosperity.

2

... But Tough People Do!

Knute Rockne said it: "When the going gets tough, the tough get going." When the roads are rough, the tough rise to the occasion. They win. They survive. They come out on top!

People are like potatoes. After potatoes have been harvested they have to be spread out and sorted in order to get the maximum market dollar. They are divided according to size—big, medium, and small. It is only after potatoes have been sorted and bagged that they are loaded onto trucks. This is the method that all Idaho potato farmers use—all but one.

One farmer never bothered to sort the potatoes at all. Yet he seemed to be making the most money. A puzzled neighbor finally asked him, "What is your secret?" He said, "It's simple. I just load up the wagon with potatoes and take the roughest road to town. During the eight-mile trip, the little potatoes always fall to the bottom. The medium potatoes land in the middle, while the big potatoes rise to the top." That's not only true of potatoes. It is a law of life. Big potatoes rise to the top on rough roads, and tough people rise to the top in rough times.

Tough times never last, but tough people do.

Possibility thinking works. It worked for my father, it has worked for me, and I've seen it work for men and women who heard me preach it. I preached it, they practiced it, and here is what happened.

Mary Martin

As I was working on this book, I received a beautiful letter from a person I had never met but had admired from a distance. Six times Mary Martin's picture has appeared on the cover of *Life* magazine. America loved her as Peter Pan, flying across the stage on Broadway, as Nellie Forbush in "South Pacific," and as Maria Von Trapp in the original Broadway production of the "Sound of Music."

I saw her as a person who was always positive, joyous, optimistic, and happy.

I never understood or knew the personal tragic paths she has walked quietly and has faced prayerfully. Then an unexpected letter from her arrived.

"Three times in the past nine years your ministry has deeply changed my life," she wrote, adding, "I'd like a chance to tell the world about it sometime."

I responded. She invited me to lunch and told me her story. I asked her if she would mind if I shared it in this book. Here it is:

"The principles of possibility thinking that I heard from your television ministry helped me accept the loss of my beloved husband, Richard Halliday, nine years ago. That was a tough time, believe me!

"Then I lost my voice and was unable to sing. That was like losing my life. Then one morning a possibility-thinking message inspired an idea that led me to health again. My singing voice returned!"

Sparkling with joy as she shared the event, she looked as young and attractive at sixty-nine as she must have looked when she was a bright, young starlet beginning her career. I could hardly believe that she had come out of the hospital only weeks before, following a car crash that had claimed one life and almost two others.

I had seen her interview on the "Today" show not long before, and she had walked with a walker. After all, she had broken her pelvis in two places and had come dangerously close to death. Now, having celebrated her sixty-ninth birth-

*Tough
times never
last . . .
but tough
people do!*

day, she had not only recovered, she walked without a limp!

"Of course, I have some trouble with arthritis and cataracts," she laughed heartily. Her eyes twinkled and flashed with exuberance and youthfulness, almost belying her confession.

Then she told me the terrible story of the accident as it had happened a few months before. She, along with her dearest female friend, Janet Gaynor, and her dearest male companion and manager, Ben Washer, had stepped into a cab in San Francisco.

"Ben insisted, 'Please get in first, Mary.' I obliged. 'You're next,' Ben said to Janet, who slipped in the middle of the back seat. Then Ben, like a gentleman, followed and closed the door behind him. Because of this seating arrangement, Ben bore the immediate impact of the speeding car, driven by a drunken driver who ran a red light. The impact was horrible! Ben was killed and Janet spent month after torturing month lingering near death, finally recovering enough to be able to return home to Palm Springs for Christmas.

"I think maybe that was one of my toughest times," Mary Martin said. Without losing the twinkle, she continued, "But as you say, tough times never last, but tough people do. And I'm a tough Texan, you know!"

What gives some persons the power to fight on after the loss of a precious loved one, after experiencing torturing physical pain day after day? There is no substitute for deep abiding faith. If we hold on, we will win out! Unquestionably the profound faith and the beautiful providence of God produce a strong and unquenchable optimistic mental attitude.

"Richard Rodgers told me that he wrote the song, 'Cockeyed Optimist' for me!" Mary spoke softly, humbly; yet she was very pleased. She continued, "He was writing the play, 'South Pacific' and he said to me, 'Mary, when I knew you'd be playing the part of Nellie, I simply thought about you and wrote these words: I'm only a cockeyed optimist. I am stuck like a dope with a thing called hope and I can't get it out of my head.'"

That's the spirit that heals all diseases, redeems lives from destruction, and brings sunshine back after the rain: Tough people have it. And they can weather the worst storm. They can rough out the toughest times. They win! They come out on top.

Benno Fischer

I met Benno Fischer in 1960, in the Richard Neutra architectural office where he served the prestigious Los Angeles firm as one of the associate architects. Richard Neutra, Benno Fischer, and I spent many days together, sketching the architectural dream church.

I noticed "KL" tattooed in bluish letters, one inch high, on Benno's left hand. Beneath it were tattooed eight numbers, each approximately one-quarter inch high.

"What does the *KL* stand for, Benno?" I asked. Surprised, he looked at me: "You mean you don't know?"

I said, "No, really. What does the *KL* stand for?"

"Oh," he said. "It stands for *koncentration larga*. That's German for *concentration camp*."

And then he unfolded his story!

It took place in Warsaw, Poland, in 1939. Benno Fischer and his sweetheart, Ann, were in love and were planning their marriage when the German army took the city. In the terrible confusion that followed, Benno was loaded on a truck and was taken, along with other Jews, to a concentration camp where he would be confined until 1945.

"Where's my Ann?" he wondered those first days—which eventually stretched into tormenting weeks and horrifying months.

Unknown to him, Ann, hearing of the impending disaster that was falling upon her city, had slipped through dark alleys. In disguise, she managed to slip out of Germany by successfully passing herself off as a non-Jew. She assumed Benno was dead.

But Benno was one of four thousand Jews in the concentration camp, each of whom was offered a daily cube of bread and a bowl of soup. The soup, of course, was far more satisfying. It extended the stomach and relieved the painful empty feeling that a cube of bread hardly satisfied. Trading bread for soup became, for many inmates, a major activity of the day. Benno was offered cubes of bread by more than one fellow inmate. He always agreed to the transaction.

As the time of the liberation approached, the camp's population dwindled from four thousand to four hundred. In a desperate effort, the Nazi Gestapo tied the feet of the remaining prisoners to each other and led them off on a long, cold march through the snow of the late winter season. Emaciated and disease-ridden, many dropped from exhaustion and were left to freeze in the snow.

Then came that unforgettable morning! A rumble of heavy engines was heard from over the hill. Then on the horizon there appeared tanks, approaching quickly through the melting snow. GI's with American flags overtook the pitiful, tragic cordon of surviving Jews. Benno Fischer was set free!

Freedom! Benno's first act was to search for his beloved Ann. Was she dead? Was she alive? "I heard someone say he thought he saw her in Stuttgart," he was told by another survivor.

On a long shot, he went to Stuttgart. While riding a bus through the city, he suddenly recognized a lovely young lady standing on the corner. He jumped off and whirled her around. He looked at her. She stared at him. In the depth of their eyes, they recognized the love that would not die.

"Ann?" Benno said.

"Benno!"

They embraced; they cried; they laughed; they loved; they survived. And they came to America! *Tough times never last, but tough people do!*

Judy Hall

In July 1980, Judy Hall, mother of two young teen-age daughters, found herself unemployed. Divorced and without steady income, Judy wondered how she would possibly survive. She had no formal education and no skill that she could call upon.

She was living in Minneapolis, Minnesota, listening to our television program as we urged her week after week to be a possibility thinker. She heard such suggestions as: "Open your mind to God. Ideas will flow in. One of these will be the idea that God means for you to grab hold of."

Judy believed what she heard. So, she decided to try real estate. But she couldn't have picked a worse time to enter the business. As a result, she failed. She could have easily gotten discouraged, but she didn't.

Her next idea was to "take the girls back to their birthplace where they can get acquainted with their heritage." She scraped together enough dollars to pack up herself and her two daughters and return to the state of their birth—Hawaii.

After returning to Hawaii, she wanted the comfort of a muumuu, the loose-fitting dress of the Islands, but also a garment with enough style to be worn to non-Hawaiian events. As she shopped for such a muumuu, she discovered that all of them were sold "off the rack" in one size. All had a similar Hawaiian print, and none really had any distinctive design. And because they were made of the Hawaiian printed fabrics, they really didn't fit any social occasions that were not Hawaiian in tone and spirit.

She suddenly remembered hearing the lesson taught in all the possibility-thinking literature. "The secret of success is to find a need and fill it." Judy saw a need and decided to fill it. She purchased some fabric in a "mainland" print and proceeded to make for herself a muumuu with a decorative border at the hem. She customized the fit so that it was comfortable but not so loose-fitting as to lose all sense of line and design. The final result was something very distinctive.

Her landlord's wife loved Judy's muumuu.

"Can you make me one?" she asked.

"Of course," Judy said, "I'd love to. When can I take your measurements?"

"Measurements?" she said. "You mean it's tailored to fit me? A muumuu tailored to fit me?" the wife asked.

"Of course," Judy said, "I specialize in custom-made, hand-tailored muumuus. The sleeves should match the length of your arms. The length and the width of the shoulders should be tailored for you."

Beyond a doubt, this was a totally new concept in manufacture and design of muumuus.

As Judy thought about the muumuus she had made, she remembered what we teach in our possibility-thinking lectures: You can test an idea to see if it will be successful or not by asking four questions.

The first question is: Is it practical and will it fill a vital human need? Judy realized a muumuu is exceptionally practical because it fits any lady, of any shape. Anyone with weight problems can easily hide bulges under the full and flowing style of the muumuu.

The second question: Can it be done beautifully? Judy thought, *Yes, the muumuu can have a greater fashion flare. It can be done with more sophisticated draping and tapering and with a layered look like formal dresses on the mainland.*

The third question: Can it be done differently enough so that it will stand out from all the others? She decided that it could if she didn't use Hawaiian prints. If she used fabrics that are popular on the mainland, the muumuu would not be restricted to wear at Hawaiian parties.

She asked the fourth question: Can it receive the stamp of excellence and be a little better than anything else that is being offered? Her answer was immediate to the fourth question also. Yes! This muumuu would not only be practical, beautiful, and different, but it would excel in value, quality, and style compared to the muumuus currently marketed in Hawaii! With one hundred dollars and this confidence she decided to start.

"Dr. Schuller," Judy Hall told me recently, "I made my first muumuu ten months ago. Today I'm turning out 123 dresses a month!"

"But are you really making money? I know you need to!"

"You bet I am!" she answered. "I'm doing it by keeping my overhead down to almost nothing. I take the measurements.

I buy the fabrics—only three basic ones, so I'm not stuck with a lot of fabric and inventory that isn't being sold. I deliver the fabric and the measurements to a lady who cuts the entire dress in her house. She works as an independent contractor. Therefore, I don't have to have a payroll. I don't have to make the payroll deductions and have all of the expensive accounting that goes along with it.

"I pick up the cut-out pieces and deliver them to one of several women who do the sewing in their homes. Because they, too, are independent contractors, I don't have the problem of overhead.

"As a result, I've been able to run this entire business, manufacturing 123 dresses a month, without any office at all. I operate out of my little apartment.

"However," she added, "my business has grown so much that we are moving to a new office next week. It will be one hundred seventeen square feet!"

I couldn't believe it. "One hundred seventeen square feet? But that's only one room, less than ten feet by twelve feet."

"Yes," she said to me, "that's all I need. Because all of the cutters and all of the seamstresses work out of their homes, I don't have the overhead or expense that go along with maintaining a factory building. I don't have the expenses of a payroll. My overhead is virtually nothing."

"But you still needed cash to finance the beginning of your operation, didn't you?" I asked.

"No," she said. "I really started with only one hundred dollars and the idea. The idea was that if people were having a muumuu tailor-made for them, then I could expect and ask for an advance payment along with their order. The deposit made with the order covers the upfront capital outlay.

"Guess what, Dr. Schuller?" she said. "You're right! Anything is possible if you have faith. And I'll tell you something else. The biggest problem any of us ever face is our own negative thinking.

"When my friends saw me with my two children and no income, they really worried about how we were going to survive. When I told them I was going to go into the dressmaking business, with my own brand and design of muumuus, they laughed at me. They said, 'You're going to try to sell muumuus to Hawaiians? Why don't you go to Alaska and sell snow to the Eskimos? Don't you know that there are tens of thousands of muumuus hanging on the racks of all of the hotel shops, dress shops, and tour centers in Hawaii today? Don't you know there is a recession going on?'

"Those were the comments I heard, but guess what?" she said enthusiastically. "I just received an order to make all of the muumuus for the two hundred girls in the graduating class of one of the largest high schools in Honolulu. It is customary for the senior girls to wear muumuus on their graduation day. For years and years and years, the muumuus have been ordered from another old Hawaiian dressmaking firm. But they were so impressed with my fashions and style and distinctive quality of manufacturing that they have placed their entire order with my firm.

"My next step is to start selling them on the mainland," she said. "After all, the mainland hasn't really discovered the muumuu because the design and the fabric haven't been correct. But I've learned what works and how to do it and I'll be selling them all over the United States of America. And do you know what, Dr. Schuller? They won't call them muumuus; they'll call them 'Judi-muu's!'"

"But, Judy," I said, "didn't you have special training for this somewhere along the line? Where did you study dress designing?"

"Oh, no, I never studied dress designing. I never studied any kind of designing. I just designed it to fit myself. You see, Dr. Schuller, I was once very heavy. I've lost sixty-five pounds! I decided I wanted a dress that would fit me and fit me well! I designed it according to my own needs."

If a single, divorced mother of two children, with no money and no special training, is able to invade a surplus market with a new product and a new concept and develop a super successful enterprise, then it's probably possible for you to create employment opportunities for yourself.

It works! Believe me! Tough times never last, but tough people do!

John Prunty

John Prunty was known throughout his community as "the roadrunner man," for in 1965, running had not become the popular endeavor it is today. There were the usual guffaws and good-natured chiding during his early morning jaunts. On June 6, 1973, John took his usual twenty-one-minute run, not knowing it would be his last.

Later that morning, John, along with the rest of the five-member construction crew, scrambled onto the roof of a small home. It was one of those hot, oppressive days, and the work was difficult. John was atop a scaffold when his foreman called to him for a tool. In reaching for it, John stepped forward, and instantly a cinder block pulled loose and gave way under his weight.

John fought the impulse to jump, thinking that he could regain his balance and avoid breaking an ankle on the uneven turf some ten feet below. But it was too late. John was already airborne and out of control from his momentum. He seemed to float, as if in a suspended weightless state, similar to flying in outer space.

His flight ended with terrible finality. His 160 pounds landed with full force upon his head, and as John tells it:

"I still shudder when I recall the sickening, grinding sound of crunching vertebrae as they snapped under the strain. My body's trajectory, coupled with its momentum, tried to force my forehead against my chest in pretzel-like fashion. Instantly I was aware I had lost feeling in my legs.

"Waves of fear, anger, and utter frustration assaulted me in those first seconds, as my immediate efforts to get up proved futile. Only my head would respond to my brain's commands. I heard a yell from above: 'Hey, John's fallen!' I alternately cursed and prayed. I turned my head to the left and saw, a few inches away, a pair of booted feet, toes facing me, which looked grotesquely like my own. 'That's strange,' I thought, 'my legs are outstretched!' But they weren't, and the subsequent realization was terrifying.

"I felt no pain until someone lifted my head slightly to

place a pillow under it. Then the pain was so severe that I had to request him to remove the pillow. I felt as if my head were suspended only by a thread. Every time I rotated it, even slightly, the pain increased and gave me the weird idea that the thread would break and my head would detach. I struggled to stay conscious.

"Surprisingly soon, the rescue squad arrived and efficiently went about preparing to place a stretcher beneath me. I dreaded the move, for by now the pain had become quite severe. I was comforted, however, by the squad's professionalism as they reassured me and tried to minimize the effects of my trauma.

"Once inside the ambulance, I began to feel a little better, comforted by the belief that I would soon be in the care of experts who would set everything straight.

"At the hospital, the neurosurgeon who took my case had me lifted onto an X-ray table. He then climbed up on hands and knees to pull and tug at my head to achieve the needed angles for pictures. Though I had known pain before, I was sure I had never experienced anything like this. A short time later the doctor brought me the unhappy confirmation that my neck was indeed broken, between the fifth and sixth cervical vertebrae. I had learned to pray as a child, so now once again I turned to God and prayed for strength to endure whatever was ahead in life's uncertain road.

"The night seemed interminable, and I spent agonizing hours reliving the outrageous events of the day, over and over again.

"But through the pain and confusion of a traumatic, potentially mortal, and life-changing injury came the memory of the words from our wheelchair president, Franklin D. Roosevelt: 'All we have to fear is fear itself.' Following that was a positive reaction—a rededication and reaffirmation of love. There were prayers of supplication to God, whose master plan undoubtedly was to unfold in the coming days; and there were prayers of thanksgiving for life that had been preserved for another endeavor.

"But the real battle was yet to come!

"I was abruptly reminded, when I awoke, of the 'tongs' which protruded from both sides of my head. The more quietly I lay, I soon discovered, the less the pain. I felt as if I were wrapped like a mummy from the chest down. That was frightening because it meant the feeling was gone. There were gadgets and meters all around me. A nurse, whom I assumed to be virtually omniscient and omnipotent, seemed to have the power to intervene at a moment's notice if anything went awry. I had never before been hospitalized, and the entire environment was foreign to me. It was like living out a novel I must have read at some time or another."

During the following weeks, it became more apparent that the major effects of John's injury would be permanent. He continued to hold out hope, though, that a miracle would occur and mend the spinal cord to the extent that it could again process messages—any message—from the brain.

With this in mind, John began to concentrate on recovery. He became interested in discovering as much as possible about just what it was he needed to recover from. He didn't even have to ask, for one day John overheard one of the nurses commenting to an aide, in reference to him, "That's the way quadraplegics are!" John had never before seen a quadraplegic. In fact, he could not spell the word, though suddenly he was one!

In that moment of truth this young husband and father knew he was a quadraplegic, a victim of a broken neck, paralyzed from the neck down for life!

But he was alive! It was a tough time . . . but no one's tougher than John.

He said, "I decided to be a survivor. In fact, three D's became my guiding theme . . . desire, dedication and determination. I knew I needed to generate and sustain the *desire* to live, to heal, and to recognize my true potential. Then I had to *dedicate* myself to that concept. *Determination* alone would give me the victory. I resolved never to surrender!"

Today, after more than eight years in a wheelchair, John claims that life is every bit as good as ever.

He says, "I know there is no place in my life for recrimination, bitterness, or hate. I fervently believe that to hate is to destroy. I want instead to love and, in so doing, to demonstrate that, regardless of body impairment, the heart retains its divinely ordained function. I recognize now that the truly handicapped are those who measure beauty by the sole prerequisite of physical perfection.

"I decided my accident was something I could never escape from. It would become a millstone around my neck, or if I practiced possibility thinking, I could turn my millstone into a milestone! I decided to do just that! I have accepted *me* as I *am* rather than as I *wish* I were. I need but to smile or wink at a wide-eyed child in the supermarket, as I buzz down the aisles in my electric wheelchair, to elicit a comment like one youngster made recently: 'Gosh, you're lucky!' "

John does more than wink or smile at children. Today he manages his own business, serving surrounding hotels and his community with a professional baby-sitter placement service. He also gives many hours as a volunteer counselor in the NEW HOPE crisis telephone counseling center in the Crystal Cathedral. Because of the new hope he has found, he is able to give new hope to the discouraged people he counsels.

John Prunty's a winner. He's a survivor, because he knows that *"Tough times never last, but tough people do!"*

Sundo Kim

I met him here in California, though his home was in Korea. My first visit to that country was right after the Korean War. Never have I seen such a bleak, barren, and defeated land. Not a single tree, shrub, or other greenery graced the landscape.

All living vegetation had been consumed in order to preserve human life. Even the trees had been stripped and cut down. The leaves were eaten as a vegetable. The bark was boiled until it became a thick, black soup. Then the bare stems and trunks were burned to provide warmth in the subzero weather. Those were tough times in Korea!

Among the crowd of impoverished refugees who fled from the North were throngs of Christians. These Christians believed in a God who would never forsake those who never forsook Him. So they held on to their hope in God. One young Korean minister from that impoverished land received a scholarship to Fuller Seminary in California. While he was studying there, we invited him to be our guest at an institute held at our church.

Imagine how impressed this young man must have been when he walked onto these church grounds with the thirteen-story tower and saw the large modern sanctuary with fountains! He heard and believed what we taught at our institute: "Believe it and you can achieve it." So he took pictures of the tower and pictures of the church. He began to dream that someday he could build a church like that in Korea.

Four years ago, I returned to Korea. When this minister heard I was going to be there, he asked me to speak in his church. All he had was a tent, but he and his people were excited. I said I'd be honored to preach for him in his tent on Saturday night.

But Saturday morning, the telephone call came. My daughter, Carol, had been seriously injured in a motorcycle accident. My wife and I got on the first plane, so I wasn't able to keep my commitment. My friend had to tell about a thousand people that I would not be able to be there as they had thought.

Just a few weeks ago, I returned to Seoul, Korea, to receive an honorary degree from Hangyang University. When my young minister friend heard that I would be in Korea, he said, "Dr. Schuller, four years ago you promised to speak at my church. You broke the promise—for a good reason—but this time you must stop and see my church." Although I was scheduled to be in Korea for only forty-eight hours, I promised him that somehow I would make it to his church.

I was amazed when I arrived in Korea. The difference the past four years has made is incredible. We flew into a beautiful airport that is a spectacular piece of architecture. Surrounding the whole airport is a glorious park of lawns, trees, and waterfalls. In downtown Seoul, a beautiful hotel has been reconstructed. It is so elegant that the sidewalks in front are of polished granite and the circular driveway is veneered in ceramic tile. As we drove down the magnificent new freeway that slices through Seoul, I saw it! Looming in the sky was a replica of our Garden Grove, California, Tower of Hope—fourteen stories tall, with a cross on top! And next to it was a glorious church building with four thousand seats. This was the Methodist minister's church!

The young pastor greeted me and must have seen how shocked and thrilled I was. He showed me through his church, introduced me to his elders and deacons, and shared with me that he has over twelve thousand members. I said, "That's amazing! That's wonderful!"

He had learned this lesson too: *"Tough times never last, but tough people always do!"*

It is amazing what God can do if we will give Him a little time to work His plan out!

In four years' time (1978–1982) a band of one thousand poor Christians moved from a tent on an abandoned acre of ground in Seoul, Korea, to a four-thousand-seat cathedral. Today they are the world's largest United Methodist church!

Carol Schuller

In the same four-year period we watched our daughter, Carol, move from a hospital bed to the ski slopes.

When we arrived from Korea to Carol's bedside in Sioux City, Iowa, after her motorcycle accident, I was shocked. She lay in her bed in intensive care. Her body was bruised, broken, and disfigured. But her spirits were whole and healthy.

On the long trip back, I had searched for my opening line. What would my first words to her be? She solved the problem by speaking first: "I know why it happened, Dad. God wants to use me to help others who have been hurt."

It was this spirit, this positive attitude, that carried her through seven months of hospitalization, intravenous feedings, and consequent collapsed veins. This positive attitude gave her the courage to fight a raging infection that threatened her limb and her life. She hung on until a new drug was released by the FDA. It was the right drug at the right time— a real miracle.

It was that same positive attitude that helped Carol make the transition from hospital patient to a "handicapped" member of a family and school. It helped her feel normal and whole again.

She refused to allow the inconvenience of an artificial limb to keep her from pursuing the active life she loved, including softball. The last picture we have of Carol with both legs is one taken when she was in her softball uniform. The athlete of the family, Carol loves to play softball.

The summer after her accident, she shocked me by saying, "Dad, I'm going to sign up for softball again this year."

"That's great!" I responded, not wanting to discourage her.

At that time, Carol's artificial leg was attached just below the knee. She was plagued by a stiff knee that could barely bend at a thirty-degree angle. She walked very stiffly. Running was out of the question.

However, I took her to the local school where all the parents were lining up with their girls to sign up for the girls' softball team. Carol signed up and went to check out her uniform.

As she swung her stiff plastic leg into the car and rested her jersey, socks, and cap in her lap, I turned to her and said, "Carol, how do you expect to play ball if you can't run?" With flashing eyes, she snapped back at me, "I've got that all figured out, Dad! When you hit home runs you don't have to run."

My daughter is tough. She's a survivor. I want you to know

that she hit enough home runs that season to justify her presence on the team!

Carol has learned the lesson too. *Tough times never last, but tough people do.* She has had six surgeries since that first amputation. Today she is skiing and has met her goal, which was to win a gold medal in the qualifying races that, in turn, admitted her to that elite corps of skiers participating in the National Ski Championships! In March 1983, she pulled her goggles on and took her place among the champions in the country—at the young age of eighteen years! Yes, she still walks with a limp. She draws curious looks from strangers. But her positive attitude helps her even with that.

Last summer my family and I were privileged to be the guests of the American-Hawaiian Steamship Company on a one-week cruise of the Hawaiian Islands. It was absolutely beautiful! On this cruise, it is customary on the last night to have a talent show in which any of the passengers can participate. Carol, then seventeen years old, surprised us one day by saying, "I'm going to be in the talent show tonight."

Now Carol doesn't sing, and of course she doesn't dance. So, naturally, I was curious as to what she would do that night. Carol is not in the least ashamed to be seen in shorts or swimming attire, although her present artificial left leg covers her stump to just below the hip. But she is very conscious of the fact that people look at her out of the corners of their eyes and wonder what happened to her.

On Friday evening, the night of the talent show, my wife and I sat in the lounge along with six hundred other people. The talent show was scheduled to take place on the stage in the big, glorified cocktail lounge. As you can imagine, it's a very secular scene. The acts that were performed that night were typical of amateur talent shows. Then it was Carol's turn.

She came on stage wearing neither shorts nor Hawaiian garb, but a full-length dress. She looked beautiful. She walked up to the microphone and said, "I really don't know what my talent is, but I thought this would be a good chance for me to give what I think I owe you all, and that is an explanation. I know you've been looking at me all week, wondering about my fake leg. I thought I should tell you what happened. I was in a motorcycle accident. I almost died, but they kept giving me blood, and my pulse came back. They amputated my leg below the knee and later they amputated through the knee. I spent seven months in the hospital—seven months with intravenous antibiotics to fight infection."

She paused a moment, and then continued, "If I've one talent, it is this: I can tell you that during that time my faith became very real to me."

Suddenly a hush swept over the lounge. The waitresses stopped serving drinks. The glasses stopped tinkling. Every eye was focused on this tall seventeen-year-old blonde.

She said, "I look at you girls who walk without a limp, and I wish I could walk that way. I can't, but this is what I've learned, and I want to leave it with you: It's not how you walk that counts, but who walks with you and who you walk with."

At that point she paused and said, "I'd like to sing a song about my friend, my Lord." And she sang,

> And He walks with me,
>   and He talks with me
> And He tells me I am His own,
> And the joy we share
>   in our time of prayer
> [originally, "as we tarry there"]
> None other has ever known.[1]

"Thank you."

There was not a dry eye, not a life that wasn't touched that night. *Tough times never last, but tough people always do!* Because tough people know that with men it may appear impossible, but with God *all things are possible!*

*It's impossible
to fail totally
if you dare
to try.*

What makes a person survive and thrive? Why are some people tough enough to win over their tough times? These questions have never before been as important as they are today because we are going through some of the toughest times that our country has ever faced. We cannot merely talk about strategies for success. We have to get down to hardcore principles that will work. And the only principles that we can believe in are principles that are tested, tried, and proven.

Many of you who are reading these words do not have time to experiment. Your energies and your resources are running out. You have to be assured that the next thing you try will not be some wild and reckless whim.

Possibility thinking works. It has helped countless people survive really tough times. It can help you too! Because possibility thinking is not just a vague attitude. It is a hard-core principle. In this book I will show you specifically how possibility thinking can get you through the hard time you are going through. Your life can also be the portrait of a survivor. You can make it. You can win, if you carefully follow the possibility-thinking plan outlined in the following chapters. The first step will be to put your problems in proper perspective. Sure, you have problems. They may be the worst you've ever faced. But chances are, they are not the worst thing that could possibly have happened. No matter how bad it is, it could always be worse. Be glad it's not. Put your problem in proper perspective. Stop making a mountain out of a mole hill.

Everybody has problems. No life is problem-free.

Now you must learn to solve and manage problems. And there is not necessarily a solution for every problem; however, every problem can be managed positively. In Chapter 4 of this book are specific guidelines on how to manage your problems creatively. To do so, it is necessary to take charge and control of your problems.

Now "to manage" means "to control." Too many people lose control of their life by surrendering leadership to outside factors. We will discuss the many factors that can inadvertently take over the leadership spot in your life.

Who is in control of your life? You can be in control yourself if you will follow the Ten Commandments of Possibility Thinking. Many suggested solutions to our problems may appear impossible. Consequently too many solutions are thrown away and never given a chance. The Ten Commandments of Possibility Thinking can show how you can make the most of the ideas that God will give you.

How does God give ideas? I've received most of the ideas that have solved my seemingly unsolvable problems through a game I call, "Count to ten and win." It's amazingly simple, but it can change your life! I will share how in Chapter 7.

Next, after you've explored and applied these principles, then you'll need to put faith to work. I'll outline for you faith's five phases to get you going. People who win over tough times are people who never stop believing. They have faith in themselves and their Lord and in the ideas that God gives them. These winners, survivors, pray for God's guidance and when they know what it is they have to do, then they take action. They do something about it. To help you get going, the entire last part of this book is dedicated to an Alphabet for Action. These times we're going through are tough, but if you are going to get through them, it's up to you. You must begin to act.

You say, "But that's easy for you to say, Dr. Schuller; these ideas, these principles work for others. They have education. They have alternatives. They have capital. They are not in my situation."

I say to you: you can do anything you want to do. You can be anything you want to be. You can go anywhere from where you are—*if* you are willing to dream big and work hard.

Have you ever heard of the story of the three negative women who lived in the bayou? They complained every day, "We've got it bad living in this bayou. No opportunity here. Others are living in the city where they have unlimited opportunities. Us, we got nothing." This is the complaint they lived their lives by, until one day a positive-thinking woman came along. After listening to the complaints, she said,

"Nonsense! Opportunity? You want opportunity? You got opportunity. You live on the bayou. The bayou leads to the river. The river leads to the gulf. The gulf leads to the ocean. You can go anywhere from where you are!"

These are tough times you're going through, but if you're going to get through, it's up to you. Ready to go? Get ready to make your dreams come true!

PART
II

*Here's How You
Can Be Tough Too!*

3

Put Your Problem in Proper Perspective

What is the secret ingredient of tough people that enables them to succeed? Why do they survive the tough times when others are overcome by them? Why do they win when others lose? Why do they soar when others sink?

The answer is very simple. It's all in how they perceive their problems. They look at problems realistically and practically. They understand the six principles that pertain to *all* problems.

What are these principles? If you knew them, understood them, and practiced them, would you, too, be a winner, a survivor? You bet! Here they are. Listen carefully, and adopt them as your own.

1 Every living human being has problems.

What is your problem? Are you unemployed? If you're an impossibility thinker you probably think that a job would solve all your problems. The truth is that employed people have problems too. Most people who have jobs complain about the fact that they have to go to work on Monday morning.

And countless people have jobs they don't like. They are giving five days a week to unhappiness. They work to live rather than live to work. They hate their jobs. They drag their feet getting to the office or factory. And once they're there they devote a great deal of their time to negative thoughts. They focus on the unenjoyable   pects of their jobs.

Some people think their problems stem from the fact that they have to report to a boss. They falsely assume that they would be happy if they could be self-employed. It's true that they might find more enjoyment in such a working arrangement, but many self-employed people have more problems than those who work for others. They have to be concerned about employee relationships and managing personnel for maximum productivity. So you work for a boss? You may think so, but in reality you're probably not. Chances are he's working for you. Everybody's got problems—the employer as well as the employee.

Well then, what is the answer? Retirement? How many people long to reach sixty-five, planning for the day they can lie in the sun, take each day as it comes, be accountable to no one, and still have money to live comfortably? Sound like bliss? It's not, really. Retired people also have their problems. Many are bored. Not a few become very depressed soon after retiring because they no longer feel productive or useful. Many actually wish they could be back at work.

Successful people! Surely they are exempt from problems. Right? Wrong! Actually the contrary is true, for success doesn't eliminate problems, it creates new ones. Imagine you are rich enough to hire cleaning people and custodians to do all the jobs you hate. Sound wonderful? Not really.

I have friends who are super wealthy. With two hundred fifty dollars, they started a business in a little garage, manufacturing Venetian blinds for house trailers. After a year they had saved a few thousand dollars from their small profits. After a couple of years, they had parlayed that into ten thousand dollars, which they used as capital to build their first little house trailer, complete with their own custom-made Venetian blinds. Sales continued to grow, netting them a handsome sum and swelling their assets to nearly fifty thousand dollars. As the years passed, their business continued to grow solidly and expand strongly.

They moved from their simple little trailer to a larger

*If it's
going to be,
it's up to
me!*

house. A few years later they moved to the ocean-front, and then to a ninety-acre ranch where they enjoyed the comfort of many to do their housework.

Now with their fortunes nearing the hundred-million-dollar mark, they have built a home in Beverly Hills, California. And guess what! They have no servants' quarters in their new luxurious home. Why not? They are tired of the loss of privacy that comes with having servants. They are weary of the problems that come with managing hired help. They're sick of servants. They've found them to be more trouble than they're worth. And so they are now cooking their own meals and cleaning their house themselves.

Yes, every living person has problems. Even the nonstriving person has the problem of inertia. This, in turn, produces a lack of zest and enthusiasm. He lives life on a low level of physical energy, becoming bored. Boredom is hardly a state of happiness or contentment. The nonstriving person who elects to avoid problems actually creates new ones.

How about the striver? The student who is knocking himself out to get an *A* average? The mountain climber who is clawing the side of the cliff, risking life and limb, for the joy of overcoming an enormous challenge? How about the handicapped person who spends hours every day in painful exercises and rehabilitation therapy? Problems? Of course! They run the risk of failure. There is always the enormous possibility of heart-wrenching disappointment if they should lose the prize after years of training.

How about the arriver—the person who reaches the mountaintop? Doesn't this person enjoy a sense of freedom and relief from all problems? Is he not free from the problem of the boredom that plagues the nondreamer? And is he not free from the fear of failing that annoys the striver? Is it not heaven on earth to come in, in first place? To reach the top of the mountain? To be elected president of the United States?

I have had a little personal experience as an achiever. My testimony is that the arriver often has greater problems than the striver.

Certainly, it is wonderful to be an arriver, an achiever. But saying that the arriver leaves all problems behind would be an error. In my experience, I have found that the arriver has greater problems than the striver.

You could not have convinced me of that back in 1955, when I was twenty-eight. I had received a call from the Reformed Church in America to begin a new church in California. We were promised five hundred dollars in cash. We had no money, no connections, no open doors. All we had was a dream. But I learned that if you have a dream, you have everything—including an awful lot of problems! I dreamed of the day when I would reach my goals, when I would be an achiever, when I would find self-satisfaction in winning and witnessing the realization of a dream come true. I dreamed of the day I would trade my problems for a prize.

I proceeded to establish a forty-year plan. I wanted to build one of the greatest churches in the world. I believed then, and still do today, that the church is the only institution in human society that is totally committed to keeping faith alive in the hearts of men and women. Without this dynamic faith the human race is doomed.

I felt that a successful church would consist of about six thousand members. I divided forty years into six thousand members and concluded I could succeed in forty years. All I would have to do was gain one hundred fifty members a year.

I worked hard and poured my life into my church. As a result I learned that great dreams of great dreamers are never fulfilled: They are always transcended. After only fifteen years, my church reached the six-thousand-member mark. We were successful. Richard Neutra designed a beautiful church that seated fifteen hundred persons at each of the two morning services.

Doors to a television ministry opened. We began to reach more people than I had ever dared to dream possible. My goals were not only reached, they were eclipsed.

I had arrived. I was a success. Was I happy with my prize, the satisfaction that comes with a job well done? Was my life free from problems? No! The more successful we became, the more problems I had.

For one thing, success attracts people. We had more people than we could handle. Our sanctuary, which seated fifteen hundred at each service, could not accommodate everyone who wanted to come. Week after week people came, saw the crowds, grew frustrated as they looked for a parking place, and left, never even having gotten out of their cars. My heart ached for them.

We decided to handle the problem with an overflow seating section outside the church. Because Neutra had designed the building with one all-glass side overlooking a beautiful grass lawn, it was natural to set up chairs outside in sunny California. The plan worked splendidly. Many worshipers opted to sit outdoors in what we called the "garden sanctuary." Until it rained.

It was disastrous. Hundreds of people were sitting outside, with no awning, and no covering for their heads. Suddenly, in the middle of my message, a cloud came from nowhere and it began to rain—not a sprinkle, but a torrential downpour. People leaped from their seats to run for cover. But there was none. The church building was packed, and fire codes prevented us from letting them join the worshipers in the dry, sheltered church building. They had no choice. They ran for their cars. They drove away. For me it was a black day.

Meanwhile, I had reached all of my goals. I tried to sit back and enjoy my success, but soon I began to die inside. I soon discovered that the only joy of living is the joy of giving. When I didn't have any goals, I was miserable.

So I focused on human beings who were empty and hurting inside—people who needed healing. The more I focused on such human predicaments and torturing sorrows, the more we came to the inevitable conclusion that we needed a larger facility. I began to contemplate how we could increase the seating of our sanctuary. We engaged an architect and instructed him to draw up plans for knocking out the wall of our fifteen-hundred-foot auditorium. In so doing we could enlarge it to three thousand seats.

We spent two years and twenty thousand dollars pursuing that idea, only to conclude it would destroy the garden environment we had created. It would cost over a million dollars and it would be a horrendous development. Everybody agreed that this was not the solution. Over the next three years, we spent another thirty thousand dollars with another architectural firm that created a model of a building that could seat three to four thousand people and would cost four to five million dollars. We engaged professional fund-raisers, but the campaign fizzled. We failed.

After five years, fifty thousand dollars, and two architectural firms, our problem was still unresolved. One day I picked up a magazine and read an article about Philip Johnson. Somehow, I felt that he was the key to solving our predicament. I called him and asked him if he could design a building to seat three to four thousand persons. I said to him, "My only request, sir, is that it be all glass."

He was shocked. He said, "All glass?"

"Yes. *All* glass." My dream for an all-glass church stemmed from a childhood loneliness to return to the river banks of Iowa. I wanted to worship under the open sky again.

"How much money can you afford to spend on the project?" he asked.

I said, "We have a four-million-dollar corporate debt which we are amortizing responsibly over twenty years. But our cash flow allows no surplus whereby we can handle any additional corporate debt," I told him. "We have borrowed an additional two hundred thousand dollars from the bank to retain you. You'll have to come up with the kind of building that will attract its own financial support."

Three months later he delivered a six-inch plastic model of an all-glass, four-pointed, star-shaped structure that was 414 feet from one point to the other. The glass roof, which was 100 feet longer than a football field seemed to float in space. At its peak it soared twelve stories above the ground! It was stunning! Unbelievable!

Today the building is a reality. It was a solution to a problem. Of course, with the creation of the Crystal Cathedral, we inherited a whole new generation of problems.

We have encountered acoustical difficulties. All-glass

structures are a nightmare for sound technicians. It is a problem we have completely solved. But it was tough! Maintenance of the cathedral is also a monumental challenge. Do you know how many window washers it takes to keep it clean? (I hear that stock in Windex soared after the cathedral was completed.) The budget to keep a building like the cathedral operational was much more than we expected. Raising the money to keep the cathedral open and in tiptop shape is a new problem we have had to solve—and we have!

These are the problems I inherited when I solved my problem of overflow seating. Naturally, the trade-off is acceptable. I would much rather deal with maintenance and budget problems than deny people the right to worship God and find spiritual and emotional healing.

However, when the cathedral was built, and my goal reached, I once more faced the problem of a lack of goal.

What do you do to top a Crystal Cathedral? How do you handle emotional stimulation produced by the mountain peak which taunts you to scale it? If you have climbed Mt. Everest, where do you go from there? How does the president of the United States maintain purpose and excitement after he has had to step down from the lofty office?

The point is clear: Nobody is free from problems. A problem-free life is an illusion—a mirage in the desert. It is a dangerously deceptive perception, which can mislead, blind, and distract. To pursue a problem-free life is to run after an elusive fantasy; it is a waste of mental and physical energies. Every living human person has problems. Accept that fact and move on to the second principle.

2 Every problem has a limited life span.

Every mountain has a peak. Every valley has its low point. Life has its ups and downs, its peaks and its valleys. No one is up all the time, nor are they down all the time. Problems do end. They do go away. They are all resolved in time.

This principle is evident when you look carefully at history, for the history of humanity is a study in peaks and valleys. Humanity peaks at times when societies rise from decadence to a highly sophisticated state of civilization. Eventually, however, most cultures allow decay to set in. Rather than rooting out the negative influences, the human institutions adjust to the downward movement. The decline continues and accelerates until it reaches a low ebb at which point it begins the long, slow ascent once more.

History teaches us that every problem has a life span. No problem is permanent. Do you have problems? They will pass; they will not last. Your problem will not live forever, but you will! Storms always give way to the sun. Winter always thaws into springtime. Your storm will pass. Your winter will thaw. Your problem will be resolved.

3 Every problem holds positive possibilities.

"It is the glory of God to conceal a thing" (Prov. 25:2). Every problem contains secret ingredients of some creative potential either for yourself or someone else.

There are two sides to every coin. What may be a problem to someone can be a profitable business for others. For instance, rats and mice are plagues to the human world. However, the presence of rats and mice in America alone results in tens of millions of dollars in our economy. Rats and mice are responsible for thousands of jobs! Factories make mousetraps. Families are supported from the income of exterminators of such pests.

Similarly, every human problem holds possibilities for someone willing to look for them.

Bankruptcy was such a horrible experience for one man that he decided to help others who were going through it. Today he is a counselor to those who are having to declare bankruptcy.

One man's problem is another man's opportunity. Consequently, hospitals exist because people are sick. Lawyers are in business because people violate laws in a moment of weakness or ignorance. Mortuaries, cemeteries, colleges, churches, and universities all exist for the purpose of helping people through their problem times.

4 Every problem will change you.

Problems never leave us the way they found us. Every person is affected by the tough times. No one emerges from a problem untouched by tough times.

Recently I was talking to a supersuccessful salesperson. His income is in the six-figure bracket. When I inquired about his training, I was surprised to learn that his degree is in history and education.

"Dr. Schuller, the truth is that I was a very boring teacher. Because I was boring, my students were restless and I failed to communicate to them. I was a boring teacher because I was a bored teacher. My boredom rubbed off on the students. It was not a good situation. Because I had a problem with students, my contract was not renewed—actually I was fired. When the school fired me I became so angry I decided to go out and make something of myself. I went out and landed a better job."

And then he shared a gem of a line. He looked at me with flashing eyes and said, "I had to get fired before I got fired up!" He went on to explain. "Basically, I was too lethargic. My contract cancellation jolted me out of a lazy rut. I'll always be grateful that I was fired, for it made me angry enough at myself to get up and get going."

5 You can choose what your problem will do to you.

You may not be able to control the times, but you can compose your response. You can turn your pain into profanity—or into poetry. The choice is up to you. You may not have chosen your tough time, but you can choose how you will react to it.

*Never
let a problem
become an excuse.*

I remember hearing Dr. Norman Vincent Peale interviewed on national television many years ago. The interviewer asked him: "Dr. Peale, how far do you apply positive thinking?"

Dr. Peale answered: "I apply it in the areas over which I have control." He continued, "If I buy a plane and the plane crashes, I have no control over that." I thought about that for a long time.

In a subsequent meeting with Dr. Peale, I said to him, "I apply possibility thinking not only in the areas of life over which I have control but over every area of life." He looked puzzled. I explained. "Actually, Dr. Peale, we can control our reaction even when we cannot control the problem."

When you control your reaction to the seemingly uncontrollable problems of life, then in fact you do control the problem's effect on you. Your reaction to the problem is the last word! That's the bottom line. What will you let this problem do to you?

It can make you tender or tough. It can make you better or bitter. It all depends on you.

6 There is a negative and a positive reaction to every problem.

In the final analysis the tough people who survive the tough times do so because they've chosen to react positively to their predicament. This is not always as easy as it sounds.

Consider, for example, the problem of an unwanted pregnancy.

What are the options? What are the alternatives? Which "solutions" are really solutions? How do you determine which reactions are positive and which are negative?

Let me answer the last question first. The positive reaction is the one that would contribute most to the collective self-esteem of the human family. Of my options, I must choose the one that would diminish any shame that could fall upon the human family. I must choose the reaction that will ultimately make me more proud of myself as a person. Furthermore, a positive reaction would be that which would bring the greatest joy to the most people. In addition, a positive reaction would be the reaction that holds the greatest possibility of making a constructive contribution to society.

By contrast, the negative reaction would be the reaction that would be most embarrassing to myself or to the human family and would prevent any good from coming from the problem that I am facing. Based upon these positive principles of choosing the most positive reaction to a problem, I have long advocated that an unwanted pregnancy should be allowed to go full term and the child should be allowed to be offered as an answer to the prayers of a childless family. Abortion is a negative solution to a problem.

How do these principles for choosing the most positive reaction to a problem apply to other problems?

For instance, what is the positive reaction to a terrible financial setback? In this situation would it be the positive reaction to cop out? Run away? Escape through alcohol, drugs, or suicide?

No! Such negative reactions only produce greater problems by promising a temporary "solution" to the pressing problem.

Stealing money in order to pay your bills is a negative solution because it will (a) generate a whole new set of problems, (b) fill you with the fear of exposure and detection, (c) haunt you with shame and rob you of your self-dignity, and (d) lower the collective self-esteem of the human family.

The positive solution to a problem may require courage to initiate it. It takes courage to face up to your creditors and to deal with them honestly and forthrightly. If they insist on pressing for payment and refuse to give time for you to resolve your position more favorably, then choose the legal and honorable route of filing for bankruptcy. This will provide the breathing space to work out your solutions without committing a crime.

Next, let's consider the problem of a troubled, quarrelsome marriage. For years it has been assumed that it is better for a child to live in peace with one parent than to live in a home with father and mother who argue frequently. Based on that unstudied, unscientific, generally accepted assumption, hundreds of thousands of married couples have chosen divorce as a swift and immediate solution to their problems of marital unhappiness. Many have sincerely believed that this is better for the children.

However, recent studies indicate that this may be, in fact, the more negative solution.

"If children ruled, there would be no divorce." So Dr. Albert A. Solnit reported to the American Academy of Pediatrics recently. This Yale University psychiatrist continued, "We do not in any sense know what the long-term effect of divorce is on children. If we were living in a world governed by children's wishes, there would be no divorce."[1]

Another child psychiatrist said there is no way he could be convinced that children were better off when parents divorce.

Dr. Derek Miller, a Northwestern University professor of psychiatry and head of the adolescent unit at Northwestern Memorial Hospital in Chicago, said there is no proof a child brought up by a single parent feels more secure and is better off than a child brought up by two parents.

He took note of a rise in suicides among adolescents, drug abuse, teen-age pregnancies, alcoholism, and even murders—problems that emerged in the sixties and grew in the seventies.

Such research indicates that it might be more positive to stay together despite the tension and arguments.

My own father and mother had quarrels. I have vivid, childhood recollections of some strong verbal arguments in our home life. But divorce was never considered. Because of this, I grew up believing that solutions are never found by running away from a tough problem.

I believe that because my parents kept their marriage intact despite problems, I am a better person and a more tenacious achiever. Their overriding, ever-recurring love taught me to believe in the importance of commitment.

---

[1]*Honolulu Advertiser*, Oct. 29, 1982, p. C-8.

If you know that divorce is not an option, it is amazing how you can learn to love again.

Tough times never last, but tough people do. Tough people stick it out. They have learned to choose the most positive reaction in managing problems. And that's the real key: "Managing problems." For in spite of all of our possibility thinking, there are after all some problems that defy solutions.

If your leg is amputated, you can't grow it back. You can manage this problem, however, by considering all the possible ways in which a prosthesis can be developed, improved, and refined. You can manage it by determining to walk better, more smoothly, more quickly than anybody else could imagine. In the process you will become an inspiration to everyone whose life touches yours.

Possibility thinking—I do not claim that it can solve every problem. But I have no doubt that the vast majority of problems can be solved if we only believe. "With men this is impossible; but with God all things are possible" (Matt. 19:26).

But if a problem defies solution, then what?

When you can't solve the problem, manage it.

Survivors. How do they do it? When they can't solve the problem, they manage it creatively. And how do you do this? By following twelve principles for managing problems creatively and constructively! We will take a look at these in the next chapter.

4

Twelve Principles For
Managing Problems Positively

The month was October. The year was 1982. Unemployment problems in America were peaking, with Flint, Michigan, hit hardest. My good friend, Tom Tipton, wanted to help the unemployed of Flint, and he asked me to conduct a two-day seminar, applying possibility thinking principles to the problem of unemployment.

Facing my audience of nearly five thousand citizens, gathered in the city's largest convention center, I asked this rhetorical question: "Are you unemployed today? Then consider this: Is your problem of unemployment really any different from any other problem? Or are there universal principles that we can apply to unemployment as to almost every other serious problem?"

I say that, yes, there are universal principles that can help manage any problem, including the problem of unemployment, that seems to defy solution. Every living human being has problems. You do too. Learn to manage them.

Are you overweight? Have you tried all kinds of diets, losing the weight only to gain it again? Have you lost a loved one through divorce or death? Have you been told that you have cancer? Do you have a problem with alcoholism? Are you facing possible bankruptcy?

If you have a problem today—any problem—I can help you if you'll let me. I offer to you the principles that I shared with my audience in Flint. They'll work if you use them.

1 Don't underestimate.

Don't underestimate the problem—or your potential power to cope with it creatively! Unquestionably, many problems are never resolved or managed effectively because they are not taken seriously enough. Have you ever been guilty of one of these thoughts?

"I'm not too fat. I don't have to worry about losing weight yet."

"I'm not getting A's or B's, but I'm passing."

"I haven't been exercising as much as I should, but I'll be O.K."

"I probably should cut down on my smoking, but I don't need to worry. Lung cancer may hit others, but I won't get it."

Such thinking is dangerous! We must avoid the temptation to underestimate the seriousness of problems that on the surface may appear slight. Problems are like a pregnancy. They will grow until their presence is obvious. No one is just a little pregnant. And no problem is unimportant enough to ignore.

Never underestimate a problem or your power to cope with it. Realize that the problem you are facing has been faced by millions of human beings. You have untapped potential for dealing with a problem if you will take the problem and your own undeveloped, unchanneled powers seriously. Your reaction to the problem, as much as the problem itself, will determine the outcome.

I have seen people face the most catastrophic problems with a positive mental attitude, turning their problems into creative experiences. They turned their scars into stars.

2 Don't exaggerate.

Instead of underestimating the problem, your instinctive (and often, first) reaction is to exaggerate it.

Are you closing your business? That isn't the end of the world. You can start over again.

Are you unemployed? It doesn't mean you can *never* get another job.

Flying back on the lonely, torturing trip from Korea to America, after Carol's motorcycle accident, I was overwhelmed with grief. I wept. I prayed.

Out of this time of deep prayer, a sentence, as clear as if it were skywriting against the clouds, passed through my mind: *Play it down and pray it up.* I took that as a direct message from God.

To me it meant this: "Don't exaggerate the problem. You're playing it up too much. She didn't lose *both* legs. She has had no head injury. She suffered no brain damage. No vital organs are permanently impaired. She is not in a life-threatening situation. You are totally exaggerating the impact of the accident. Play it down. Then pray it up. Give it to God and give God a chance to show how the scars can be turned into stars."

Are you unemployed? Are you depressed to the point that you want to stop the world and get off? Maybe you are exaggerating your problem.

Would you rather have your left leg amputated? Would you like to trade places with my daughter? My wife had her left breast removed because of cancer. Would you rather have her problem?

In my experience as a pastor, *I have never met anyone who wanted to exchange his problem for someone else's.* Put your problem in its proper perspective. The seriousness of it will pass.

Ask yourself these questions: What is the worst that will happen to me? Can I handle that?

If you will play it down and pray it up, God will give you

*The one battle
most people lose
is the battle
over the fear of failure...
try...
start...
begin...
and you'll be assured
you won the first round.*

the ability to cope with the worst that will happen. Stop exaggerating the depth, the length, and the breadth of the problem.

3 Don't wait.

There is a time and place for patience—after you have tried every avenue possible and have planted as many seeds of solutions as you can. Patience is not a virtue if you sit back and wait for your problem to solve itself.

If you are unemployed, don't expect the phone to ring or a letter to miraculously show up in your mailbox with job offers. Don't expect the government to telephone you and offer you a job. Don't expect the union to call you and offer you a job. Don't expect the company to call you and rehire you.

If such should be the case, wonderful. But merely waiting for it to happen could be the worst thing to do. And many problems have the built-in capability to grow more serious with the passing of time. To wait quietly for God to do something or for someone to come to your rescue could give the problem time to multiply its negative fallout.

During President Lyndon Johnson's administration, the federal government purchased several blocks in the South Bronx in New York City. The president announced that the many multistoried structures in this slum area would be demolished, and through government financing, a new model city would rise.

Several years after the federal government purchased the property, I visited the area. I saw the buildings still empty; windows, still shattered; the area, totally dilapidated. The situation has not changed. The South Bronx is still waiting!

To wait is to waste time and opportunity. And to wait may be to surrender leadership to forces that may never materialize.

If you want to solve your problem, don't wait for somebody else to help you. Tackle it yourself. I'll show you how in Chapter 7. *Right now, understand that you alone are personally responsible for managing your problem. Don't expect anybody else to do it for you.*

Look to God and to your own capabilities. If you expect others to rescue you, you will only be disappointed. Worse than that, you may also become cynical and bitter.

4 Don't aggravate.

We have the power to make any problem better or worse. We do this when we react positively or negatively. The normal reaction would be to feel threatened by the problem. Threatened people become angry people. Fearful people reflect hatred. Hatred and anger only aggravate the problem. They are not positive reactions. They will not help solve the problem.

So you are overweight? Don't hate yourself for eating so much. That will not help you one bit.

Unemployed? Don't hate your company for laying you off. Likewise, don't hate your country for not coming through with a job offer, or your community for having an I-don't-care attitude about the unemployed people.

Coach John Wooden chalked up a string of victories while he coached the famed University of California at Los Angeles basketball team. I once heard him say, "Nobody is defeated until he starts blaming somebody else."

My advice is, "Don't fix the blame; fix the problem." You begin fixing the problem when you begin to control your negative emotions.

One of the first pieces of advice I gave to my daughter after arriving at her wounded side was: "Carol, there is one thing you'll have to be careful of. And that is feeling sorry for yourself. Self-pity will only lead you into hell on earth."

"Don't worry about that, Dad," she replied quickly, adding, "I've got enough problems without that one."

If you've got a problem, don't add to it. Don't make your problem worse by aggravating it with self-pity, jealousy, cynicism, hatred, anger, or lack of positive faith in the future.

5 Illuminate.

Illuminate your mind. Get smart and then get smarter. Ask yourself some questions:

"Has any other person faced my problem and overcome it?"

"What really is my problem anyway?"

"Is my problem unemployment or is it early retirement?"

"Is it a lack of money to meet my needs, or is it boredom?"

"Could I solve the problem of boredom by volunteering to work in my church or community organizations?" My own father enjoyed his retirement because he was always volunteering to repair things in the houses of people who lived in his town.

If you think your problem is finances, think again. Is it really finances, or is it a problem of managing what you have? You probably need to pare down some of the expenses that you have taken for granted. Remember: Nobody has a money problem; it is always an idea problem.

My youngest daughter, Gretchen, is taking driving lessons. She will soon be sixteen and will have her driver's license. Her teacher tells her that she has to learn to drive with the IPDE method: *Identify, Predict, Decide, Execute.* Her teacher explained: "As you are driving down the street, *identify* the other moving vehicles. *Predict* what they are going to do and when they are going to do it. *Decide* how you will respond and react to their behavior. *Execute* your response decisively and forthrightly."

The IPDE prescription can help you face a variety of problems. *Identify* the problem. *Predict* what this problem will do to you if you don't do anything about it. *Decide* on your response from all of the options and alternatives. Then, *execute* and act on the most positive option that you can imagine.

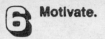

Motivate.

When you consider all of the positive reactions, you will be motivated to positive action. "It take guts to leave the ruts," I said to someone whose only solution to his problem was a major alteration in his life-style. His drinking problem was connected with a group of friends with whom he had been associating for years. "You've got to separate yourself from this crowd," I said. He followed my advice, and his problem went away.

"You don't have a problem to solve—you just have a decision to make" was my advice to another person. He had been laboring under the illusion that he had a problem, when in fact he only lacked the courage to make the right decision. Once I gave him this advice, he made the tough decision. Some wonderful people who worked for him in his company were not contributing to the company's profit. In fact, they were unnecessary drains on the payroll. It was a tough and painful decision. But when the employer realized he didn't have a problem to solve, but a decision to make, he was on his way to creative problem management.

"Every obstacle can be an opportunity" was my advice to still another person who was unemployed. "Think about that," I said, "and come back to see me in one week and give me a list of all the new opportunities that face you today that wouldn't have been yours if you were still employed." One week later he came back with this list of exciting opportunities: (1) I do have the opportunity to start my own business; (2) I do have the opportunity to travel; (3) I do have the opportunity to go back to school; (4) I do have the opportunity to give more time to my church and to my children and grandchildren.

The list was long enough to lift my friend from depression to real enthusiasm. It's not surprising that from this list emerged an idea that since has given him meaningful employment.

7 Bait.

"How do I get a job when I'm unemployed?" one person asked me.

My answer was a question: "How do you catch a moose?"

"What do you mean by that?" he asked, almost irritated.

I told him this story: "Your problem with unemployment really isn't that much different from the problem I faced a few years ago when I had to raise ten million dollars to build a new church, the Crystal Cathedral. At that time I had heard about a friend, Dr. Milton Englebretson, who successfully solicited a million-dollar donation from one individual. I went to my friend and asked, 'How do you raise a million-dollar donation from one person?' He answered me with the same question I threw at you.

" 'How do you catch a moose?' He smiled at me. He stared at me. His eyes unflinchingly met mine, in a steady, twinkling gaze.

" 'What kind of an answer is that?' I asked.

" 'You're smart,' he answered. Turning to walk away, he threw a parting comment to me, 'Think about it—that's all the advice you need.'

"I couldn't get his comment out of my mind. I didn't want his riddle to get the best of me. I thought, *Well, if I wanted to catch a moose I would go to Canada. I'd never catch one in Orange County, California. Then I would have to find out what paths they take and where they find their water. I'd have to bring the kind of food that would attract them to me. And I'd have to be able to close in.*

"So, prayerfully I made a list of persons who had the potential of giving a million-dollar gift. And as a result of that advice, we successfully collected several contributions in the million-dollar bracket.

"Now when others ask me, 'Dr. Schuller, how do you raise a million-dollar gift?' my answer is, 'How do you catch a marlin?' "

I was born and raised in Iowa, where the largest fish I ever caught was a five-pound walleyed pike. But when I came to California I learned that California fishermen caught glamorous, flying marlin, which could weigh more than three hundred pounds!

I decided that I wanted to catch a marlin sometime in my life. And I have! In the process, I learned something about catching marlins. First of all, you don't stay in Iowa; you go to where the marlin are—probably off Catalina Island in southern California or off Kona Coast in Hawaii, or in Cabo San Lucas in Baja California, Mexico. Then you get into a boat. You'll never catch a marlin from the shore or on the pier. You have to head out for the open waters, cruise, and throw out bait.

Need a job? Go to where the jobs are. And then throw out the bait. Put in your application. Put ads in the paper. Let people know you are available.

8 Date.

If you are unemployed, find a job the way you found a wife or husband. Discover the many different kinds of jobs there are. Look them over. Play the field. Don't let age be a factor; a change of career at forty may be just what you need. And don't tell yourself, "There aren't many jobs. The few that are available will be snatched up by other people who are unemployed. I don't stand a chance."

Don't get discouraged. You do have a chance. You can find the job that's best for you. Even if you called last week, call again. Every day somebody retires or quits because he is fed up with his job. And every week people decide to pack up and move to Florida, Hawaii, or California, leaving a job behind. Every month somebody burns out. So every day, every week, and every month there are brand-new job openings where there weren't any before. The person who knocks at the door, telephones, dates, and plays the field is the person who is going to get that job.

"Dating" is a principle of problem management that applies to many areas other than unemployment. It applies to loneliness, and to the problem of finding people you need to help make your company a success.

9 Sublimate.

Every problem, even yours, is loaded with possibilities. You can turn your mountain into a gold mine. Try "possibilitizing." Believe that every time one door closes, another will open. Sublimate your problem. That means believing that every adversity holds within it the seeds of an undeveloped possibility.

A young lady had been hurt deeply. Her boyfriend had treated her shabbily, then had dumped her. "God uses life's bruises if we surrender them to Him," I promised her. "In love's service only broken hearts will do." A person who is hurt can become bitter and calloused, or one can react positively and prayerfully, becoming tender, compassionate, sensitive, and profoundly caring for others who are hurt. *God uses life's bruises!* When you can't eliminate the problem, sublimate it. Turn the stumbling block into a stepping stone.

10 Now dedicate.

Most people fail, not because they lack intelligence, ability, opportunity, or talent, but because they haven't given their problem all they've got!

Anyone can succeed if he can get enthusiastic about life even when life seems empty. Doors will open to the enthusiastic person first!

I was in a hotel in Los Angeles when I ordered room service. The waiter was Mexican and spoke halting English: "Good morning! Good morning! Good morning!" Strangely enough, his repeating the greeting three times did not seem overdone, but very sincere.

"You seem enthusiastic," I offered.

"Oh, yes," he said, grinning from ear to ear. "I've got a good job. And I'm in America. May I pour your coffee for you?"

"Yes, of course," I replied.

"The weather is going to be beautiful today," he said.

"I heard they were predicting rain today."

"Yes, but the rain will be nice. It will make the lawns green. And the flowers and trees need it, don't they?"

By the time he left the room I was enormously impressed by him. *I know why he has a job*, I told myself.

The smartest and the most enthusiastic people will get the jobs that are going to be opening up in the next thirty days. Get enthusiastic. Dedicate yourself to enthusiastic living, and you'll be surprised how people will want to hire you.

I didn't say it was easy. It's not always been easy for me to step in front of the television cameras and smile enthusiastically. It's a commitment I've made to dedicate myself to being positive always—especially if I don't feel like it. And it has never failed me. The positive approach has always attracted positive support, from friends I've known a long time as well as from people I never knew before.

So your problem is not unemployment? Remember this: Unexpected sources of help come from unpredictable quarters to the person who remains positive and enthusiastic and cheerful! That's my promise.

11 Communicate.

Manage your problem by remembering that oftentimes the solution lies in help from some other source. Do you need help? Then ask for it. Don't be too proud to tell people you need help.

Our television ministry is one of the most successful in America today. At one time we were on the verge of terminating the program for lack of financial support. My advisors said, "Dr. Schuller, you have to go on national television and tell the people the truth. Tell them that you need money. You have to tell them that if you don't get the money needed that you'll have to discontinue the program."

Frankly, that hurt my pride. I had to make a decision. Did I want to be successful? Or did I want to be proud? I chose to be successful. I humbled myself by honestly telling my national television audience, "I need help." And they responded.

Every alcoholic will agree that the three hardest words to say are, "I need help!" More than one "impossible" marital problem has moved from an impasse to a creative resolution when a husband or wife has said, "Honey, you have to help me work out the negative feelings I have toward our situation. I should not have these negative feelings. I know they are wrong, but I have them. I don't want them; they hurt me and they are going to ruin both of us. Please help me."

Do you need help? Do you need hope? Are you discouraged? Depressed? Has enthusiasm waned? Do you want to quit, pack up, and run away from life? Then ask for help. Seek it out. There is hope waiting for you. Whatever else you do, *communicate*. Don't *ex*communicate yourself from the help that is available.

Proud people are inclined to withdraw. Don't reject or neglect the free hope and help that is available. Start listening to positive thinking messages. Try praying. Ask God questions. And listen for His answers. Be brutally honest when you ask Him for advice.

Do you need wisdom? Counsel? Guidance? *Go for it!* But isolating yourself from all available help will ultimately defeat you.

Try linking-thinking. Visit a church. Join a club. Get into a community group. But discipline yourself to share your dreams, your hopes, and your needs with others. You'll be surprised at how help will come to you and your problem will be managed.

12 Insulate.

Don't isolate yourself from help, but do insulate yourself from negative forces and negative personalities.

Maintaining a positive mental attitude becomes a near-impossible task if we allow ourselves to be bombarded by the negative thoughts that constantly surround us.

Check out the positive or negative content of your own conversations and the advice that people give you. Become sensitive to the widespread, taken-for-granted, negative sentences that are pumped into your brain daily by well-meaning friends. Insulate yourself from the following phrases:

1. *"Take care."* In the next chapter we teach: "People who take care never get anywhere." Managing problems requires that we take control.

2. *"Take it easy."* Of course it is important to maintain poise and calm rather than give in to panic and hysteria. What I object to is the advice that would urge us to take it easy and wait. I repeat: Don't expect somebody to just hand you the solution. Resourcefulness and creative initiative can be stifled by the take-it-easy attitude.

3. *"Thank God, it's Friday."* It is impossible to determine the extent to which productivity has declined in America because of the more than one hundred million workers that have allowed themselves to say or think, "TGIF." Obviously, enough people have thought this thought and have repeated these words to contribute to a collective reduction of enthusiasm. Enthusiasm is energy. Therefore, if you reduce the collective level of enthusiasm, you reduce energy. The work pace slows, and output per hour is unquestionably going to suffer.

4. *"I've got to see it before I believe it."* The trouble with this negative statement is that it is inside out, upside down, and backward. The truth is, "You've got to believe it before you see it!"

5. *"No way."* How many times has a positive idea been

slaughtered, strangled, or sunk with these two torpedoing words. Never repeat them. Never allow anybody to use them in your presence. There is *always* a way if people are willing to pay the price in time, energy, or effort!

6. *"Not too bad."* How many times have you asked a person how they were, only to have them answer with "Not too bad"? Basically this is a negative statement. It may appear an innocent and harmless comment, but it programs persons for emotional mediocrity. That adds up to lack of enthusiasm.

We need to insulate ourselves from such statements, as well as from a negative climate, if we are going to keep our enthusiasm at a peak.

You cannot live in a bubble. Many, many people that you meet each day will threaten to pop your bubble and drain your enthusiasm with their so-so, not-too-bad, pretty-good attitudes. I face them too. But I insulate myself by sharing with them "Schuller's Scale of Spirit."

When I ask someone, "How are you today?" their answer falls somewhere on my scale from one to ten:

1. Silence, trembly lips, eyes filled with tears.
2. Profane anger; a torrent of swear words.
3. "Awful. You would be too if you had the problems I face."
4. "Not too bad." (That's just one step above awful!)
5. "Pretty good." (That's just one step above "not too bad" and two steps above "awful.")
6. "Good."
7. "Great."
8. "Terrific."
9. "Fantastic."
10. "Sensational!"

Remember, you can control your mood. Tell yourself you *are* great. For nothing great ever happens on the "O.K." level.

7. *"I've heard that before."* This is another one of those negative cynical remarks. Avoid cynical people like a plague.

8. *"Never." "Can't." "None."* Any negative absolute is destructive. Insulate yourself from negative absolutes.

9. *"The case is closed."* So? Maybe the case can be reopened.

*God's delays
are not
God's denials.*

Maybe it can be appealed. Just because the case is closed doesn't mean you need to accept defeat.

10. *"It's terminal."* Nothing is terminal. Everything is transitional. Every end is a new beginning. Don't let phases faze you. Phases are passages. And passages are never dead ends. What looks like the end of the road will turn out to be a bend.

Tune your positive antennae to hear the difference between positive and negative statements. And insulate your mind from the negative, for solutions always lie in the positive.

Consider the following article by Barry Siegel. It shows in a light-hearted way how ridiculous it is to give in to negative arguments.

PALO ALTO, CALIFORNIA. Alarmists, worrying about such matters as nuclear holocaust and pesticide poisoning, may be overlooking much more dire catastrophes. Consider what some scientists predict: If everyone keeps stacking *National Geographics* in garages and attics instead of throwing them away, the magazine's weight will sink the continent 100 feet some time soon and we will all be inundated by the oceans.

If the number of microscope specimen slides submitted to one St. Louis Hospital laboratory continues to increase at its current rate, that metropolis will be buried under 3 feet of glass by the year 2024. If beachgoers keep returning home with as much sand clinging to them as they do now, 80 percent of the country's coastline will disappear in 10 years. Hard to believe? Scientists have the statistics and formulas to prove all this. They have even published them. Welcome to the *Journal of Irreproducible Results*, the official publication of the Society for Basic Irreproducible Results. The general public may not know about the journal but many scientists do. Published for 26 years, written and edited by scientists, the journal now has 40,000 subscribers in 52 countries. The *Journal* spoofs, parodies, and satirizes what its editor calls "the verbosity, pompous obscurantism, and sheer stupidity encountered in scientific publications and projects." Some items in the quotes are real reprints from legitimate journals to illustrate their factuality. But most articles are parodies written in technical scientific language complete with diagrams, tables, formulas, mathematical calculations and nonsensical conclusions. Far-reaching conclusions extrapolated from limited data are a favorite target of the journal. Several articles over the years have achieved the status of legend.

In "Pickle and Humbug" the journal reported the striking discovery that pickles cause cancer, communism, airline tragedies, auto accidents and crime waves. About 99.9% of cancer victims had eaten pickles some time in their lives, the article pointed out. So have 100% of all soldiers, 96.8% of Communist sympathizers and 99.7% of those involved in car and air accidents. Moreover those born in 1839 who ate pickles have suffered 100% mortality rate and rats force-fed 20 pounds of pickles a day for a month ended up with bulging abdomens and loss of appetite.

By far the most famous article the journal has carried is "*National Geographic* Doomsday Machine," written by one George H. Kaub. Kaub pointed out that more than 6.8 million issues of the *National Geographic*, each weighing two pounds, are sent to subscribers monthly and that not one copy has been thrown away since publication began 141 years ago. Instead copies are relentlessly accumulating in basements, attics, in public and private institutions of learning, the Library of Congress, the Smithsonian Institute, Goodwill, Salvation Army . . . soon the geologic substructure of the country will no longer support the load, Kaub predicted. Some subsidence will occur. Rock formations will compress, then become plastic and begin to flow. Great faults will appear. The continent will begin to sink and be inundated by the seas. In fact the increased earthquake activity in California along the San Andreas Fault that has already occurred was triggered by population growth in the state, the article said, and the subsequent increase in *National Geographic* subscriptions. Kaub ended by calling for nothing less than the immediate halt to publication of the *National Geographic* by Congressional action or Presidential edict if necessary.[1]

---

[1]"World May End With a Splash," *Los Angeles Times*, Oct. 9, 1982. Copyright © 1982, *Los Angeles Times*. Reprinted by permission.

The point of it all? The point is that negative thinking can easily produce exaggerated conclusions that are most irresponsible.

Be positive. You can solve your problems. When a problem seems to defy solution, you can manage it. You manage it when you work the twelve principles that I've shared with you. But none of this will work effectively unless you take positive control of your life and your thoughts. Let's see how to do that.

5

Take Charge and Take Control

There's a seemingly harmless phrase that has swept the country. People no longer just say, "Good-bye." They inevitably add, "Take care."

But I contend it's wrong to say, "Take care." Instead say, "Take a chance; take charge; take control!" Why? Because people who take care never get anywhere! If you want to manage your problem successfully, you need to "take a chance, take charge, take control!" Taking a chance by itself is a reckless risk. But when you take charge, you manage that risk. When you take control, you manage your problems.

Take charge, take control, and never surrender leadership. What do I mean by leadership? I'll give it to you in a sentence: Leadership is the force that selects your dreams and sets your goals. It is the force that propels your endeavors to success.

Abraham Lincoln told a marvelous story about a blacksmith who stuck a long, round iron bar in the coals until it was red-hot. Then he put it on the anvil, where he hammered it flat to make a sword. When he was finished, he was most unhappy with it. So he put it back into the red-hot coals and decided to broaden the flat part out a bit and make a garden tool. That didn't please his fancy either. He put the bar back into the coals, rounded it a bit, and then shaped it into a horseshoe. This effort also failed miserably. As a last resort, he put the bar into the coals one more time. He removed it from the hot fire, wondering if there was anything else he could make from it. Deciding that there was nothing, he merely stuck it into a barrel of water. At the resulting hiss, he said, "Well, at least I made a fizzle out of it!"

Your dreams don't have to fizzle. Your life can sizzle, and your problems can be overcome if you will take charge and take control by learning and following the dynamic leadership principles outlined in this chapter.

You would be amazed how many "leaders" are unaware of these principles. Before they know it, they lose control and are defeated by problems they should have been able to manage successfully.

Don't surrender leadership to outside forces.

In a corporate structure, leadership is not always at the desk of the president or the chairman of the board. Too often people in top positions surrender their power to outside forces.

I know this to be true. Some years ago, my congregation met in a smaller church building. Like so many other churches and corporations, we surrendered leadership to our property and our buildings. The church board was not in command. The pastor was not in command. People said, "We can't do that. We don't have enough parking. We don't have a large enough auditorium."

Then this thought came to me: The shoe doesn't tell the foot how big to grow. The body doesn't surrender leadership to the garment.

Don't surrender leadership to forces such as property, buildings, location. If you need to rebuild or relocate, take charge and take control.

Never surrender leadership to such forces as poverty. Don't allow lack of money to determine your dreams or your goals. There is always a way to raise the capital you need. You may have to save and count your pennies, but somehow the money will come. There is a universal principle that al-

*Today's
decisions
are
tomorrow's
realities.*

ways manifests itself: Money flows to good ideas; good ideas spawn other good ideas; dreams inspire creativity in money management.

There are many things we can't control. We can't control inflation. We cannot control a recession. But we can control our ideas and what we do with them.

I have a dear friend who, like many others, was caught in the depression of the thirties. He was broke, penniless. He couldn't control his poverty, but he didn't surrender leadership to the forces of the depression.

He was a salesman and not doing too well. One night, one of his fellow salesmen said, "Hey, did you hear about the guy who made so much money with Coca-Cola? You know, it used to be that the only way you could get a glass of soda was from a soda fountain. But then this guy came up with a way to bottle it. He told the Coca-Cola company that they could use his idea if they would give him a fraction of 1 percent of their increased sales. That minute percentage made him a millionaire."

That day my friend had been to the gas station because he needed oil in his car. In those days, the only way you could get oil was to go to a gas station where they pumped it out of huge drums and poured it into your car. Later that night he thought to himself, "I wonder if I could bottle oil?" Then he thought, "No, if the bottle broke, there would be a mess. But cans would work!"

So he went to a can company and said, "Can you sell me cans?" He went to a friend who owned a Pennsylvania oil well that produced so much oil he couldn't market it.

Then he went to a grocery chain and said, "I've got an idea how you can vastly increase your retail sales. I'll tell you how if you'll give me just seventy-five dollars for every freight car load of oil you sell."

They said, "O.K., what's your idea?"

"Sell automobile oil in cans. I'll provide them to you."

"Canned car oil?"

"Yes."

At only seventy-five dollars per freight car of cans, he

became a multimillionaire during the Great Depression. He used it as the base of his now-enormous financial empire.

2 Don't surrender leadership to faces.

Lots of people do that. I've seen it happen. I've done it myself. You read an audience. You see an eyebrow raise or hear a throat being cleared. Through body language, someone suggests that he may not support you. You read on his face that he's going to criticize you. He's not going to back you. He's against you. Before you know it, you have been intimidated by body language into silence and retreat. At that point you have surrendered leadership to a face.

3 Don't surrender leadership to farces.

Farces are lies, masks. Often people of Asian, African, and Spanish minority groups have been taught that they are genetically and intellectually inferior. Now that's a farce, a mask, a lie! If people say that one race is superior or inferior to another, don't you believe it!

A good friend of mine, a black man named George Johnson, has experienced racism. He grew up in Chicago, polishing shoes in a barber shop. George used to hear his black friends say, "I wish I could straighten my hair."

One day while George was shining a man's shoes, he asked him, "What do you do?"

"I'm a chemist," the man replied.

"What do chemists do?" George asked.

"I mix things," the man explained.

"Do you think you could mix something that would straighten my hair?"

The chemist said, "Maybe I can put something together."

He did. George tried it on his hair and it worked. He bottled the product and sold it to some of his friends and a few stores. Soon he built a sales force to sell "Ultra-Sheen."

Today, George Johnson's personal fortune is over several million dollars. That's not bad for someone who was once a shoeshine boy.

4 Don't surrender leadership to fences.

Fences are limiting concepts that you allow to influence your goals and dreams. Because of these concepts, we throw away ideas and dreams that we are sure we'll never be able to realize. They also cause us to lower our goals, with the result that we strive for and achieve far less than our capabilities.

These fences are negative self-image perceptions such as:

"I don't have an education."

"I don't know the right people."

"I don't have enough money."

"I'm not a member of the right organization."

Never surrender leadership to fences or locked-in thinking. Locked-in thinking is the thought process that says, "It's never worked before. Why should it now?"

Or, "This is the way it's always been done, so it must be the best." Nobody is more guilty of locked-in thinking than trained, educated professionals. They have been so disciplined, so trained that as they develop a discipline, an expertise, they also develop locked-in thinking.

The elevator at the El Cortez Hotel in San Diego couldn't handle the traffic. The experts—engineers and architects—were called in. They concluded that they could put another elevator in by cutting a hole in each floor and installing the motor for the new elevator in the basement. The plans were drawn up. Everything was in order. The architect and the engineer came into the lobby discussing it. The janitor, who was there with his mop, heard them say they were going to chop holes in the floors.

The janitor said, "That's going to make a mess."

The engineer said, "Of course. But we'll get help for you, don't worry."

The janitor replied, "You'll have to close the hotel for a while."

"Well, if we have to close the hotel for a while, we'll close the hotel. We can't possibly survive without another elevator."

The janitor held the mop in his hands and said, "Do you know what I would do if I were you?"

The architect arrogantly asked, "What?"

"I'd build the elevator on the outside."

The architect and the engineer just looked at each other.

They built the elevator on the outside—the first time in the history of architecture that an elevator was built on the outside of a building.

5 Don't surrender leadership to frustrations.

There are people who reach a point where they just can't handle people any more. They can't handle government regulations any more. They can't handle cash-flow problems any more. Anyone who has dreams and goals also has frustrations: lack of time and money, high interest rates, disappointments when your best people let you down. Such frustrations can mount up, and if you surrender leadership to them, you'll soon cash in, give up, throw in the towel, quit. Don't give in to such temptations.

6 Don't surrender leadership to your fantasies.

It's amazing. God gives you a brilliantly exciting idea, and you soon give in to negative fantasies: "I might try it and be rejected"; "People might laugh at me."

My dear friends, let me tell you something very honestly. I am not immune to such negative thoughts.

When we dreamed of the Tower of Hope and the Crystal Cathedral, two major building projects on our church campus, I wondered, "What will people say? What if we try it and it fails? We'll be the laughingstock of the country."

Let me tell you, if your dreams are bigger than most, if your ideas are more creative, there will be criticism. There will probably be some ridicule. But don't create more condemnation than is really there. Don't allow yourself to indulge in negative fantasies that limit the size of your goals and stifle your creativity.

7 Don't surrender leadership to fears.

The Bible says, "God has not given us a spirit of fear, but of power and of love and of a sound mind" (2 Tim. 1:7). That means when you surrender to fears, you can be sure the fears did not come from God. God does not give us the spirit of fear. God gives us the spirit of power and love and a sound mind.

If you have many fears, all you have to do is cure yourself of one fear, and that's the fear of failure. This will help: "I'd rather attempt something great and fail than attempt nothing and succeed."

I admire people who make a commitment, and stick their neck out. I admire a person who tries to reach the top and doesn't make it. Perhaps he is someone who declares his candidacy for public office in a sincere desire to be a public servant for community good. He can be sure that he will be criticized and condemned, and probably misinterpreted and distorted. His ego will surely take an awful beating. What does he get out of it? Even if he loses the race, he is a winner because he has conquered his fear of trying. In doing so, he has won his biggest battle. Every loser who tries to do something great is really a winner.

There is no need to fear failure. As I said in *You Can Become the Person You Want to Be:*

> Failure doesn't mean you are a failure . . . it does mean you haven't succeeded yet.

Failure doesn't mean you have accomplished nothing . . . it does mean you have learned something.

Failure doesn't mean you have been a fool . . . it does mean you had a lot of faith.

Failure doesn't mean you've been disgraced . . . it does mean you were willing to try.

Failure doesn't mean you don't have it . . . it does mean you have to do something in a different way.

Failure doesn't mean you are inferior . . . it does mean you are not perfect.

Failure doesn't mean you've wasted your life . . . it does mean you have a reason to start afresh.

Failure doesn't mean you should give up . . . it does mean you must try harder.

Failure doesn't mean you'll never make it . . . it does mean it will take a little longer.

Failure doesn't mean God has abandoned you . . . it does mean God has a better idea![1]

8 Don't surrender leadership to fatigue.

Everybody runs tired once in a while. You better be able to know when you're running tired and then back off. Because if you don't, you're going to make some bad decisions.

I'm not one who likes to give in or slow down when I'm tired. But even Jesus retreated occasionally. Do you remember the time when the multitudes pressed upon Him and He got into a boat? While they were calling to Him and reaching to Him, He left them. He just pulled away, escaped, and went to the mountains to pray.

History will long ask the question: "Did Franklin D. Roosevelt surrender leadership to his fatigue at Yalta?" He was a very sick man. The wisdom of his decisions that affected the present-day Eastern bloc countries is still being debated by historians.

There are times when you should not see people or make

decisions. When I'm tired, I often do not see people. I owe a great deal to my dear wife. She knows me very well, and she has arranged my calendar very carefully. She knows when my energies are taxed, and she blocks off time for renewal. Each year she plans mini-vacations for me immediately after busy times of the year. That way I never get burned out.

9 Don't surrender leadership to faults.

A lot of people do that. Somebody comes along with a good idea only to have someone else say, "Oh, but it will take too long, or it will cost too much." Or "Somebody else is doing it." They find fault with a good idea and annihilate it. They surrender leadership to the faults instead of to the potential. There are problems with every idea. But problems call for polishing, not for demolition. It's amazing how faults can control our lives if we let them.

I once counseled with a young person who had a problem. She said, "Everything is going wrong with my life. I'll never be able to amount to anything. It's all my parents' fault, really. They broke up. My family fell apart. Dr. Schuller, if you had my problems, you'd be where I am too."

I said to this young person, "Listen, I understand you have had problems. But let me tell you something. Never let a problem become an excuse."

When you let the problem become an excuse, you've surrendered leadership. Accept the faults, the shortcomings, and the imperfections. And then rise above them. You can if you have the right attitude. That leads me to the next principle.

10 Don't surrender leadership to facts.

The problems you are facing today may be fact, not just theory. The unemployment statistics are factual. You may recognize this truth when you collect your unemployment check. But don't surrender leadership to it. Facts, statistics, interest rates can definitely influence your life, but you can choose whether or not the influence will be beneficial or detrimental.

Dr. Karl Menninger, one of the great psychiatrists, made one of the wisest statements I've ever heard: "Attitude is more important than facts." Your attitude needs to remain positive and in the control position. Never let yourself be defeated by the facts.

11 Don't surrender leadership to frenzies.

A lot of people maintain control and they make the right decisions until they get into a frenzy, a frantic situation. This past week, as I was flying east, a gentleman on the plane waved at me as if he recognized me. I asked, "Do we know each other?"

He said, "You don't know me, but I know you. I watch 'Hour of Power' all the time."

I sat down. We chatted. He was Bob McClure, an airline captain. He said, "I fly the L1011. I've been a pilot for twenty-seven years."

I said, "If you've been a pilot for twenty-seven years, you must have a good story. What is the most unusual thing that's ever happened to you?"

He said, "During the Second World War, I was a solo fighter of an F6 Hellcat. I was on a first-bombing, strafing mission over Tokyo Bay. I took off from the aircraft carrier. I was to come in at a high elevation and make a deep, deep, strafing dive leveling out at three hundred feet above the bay."

Now three hundred feet is not very high.

He said, "I was coming down at an astronomical speed. And just as I started to level off, the left wing took a direct hit. It tipped my plane completely upside down."

I said, "Did you know that you were upside down?" (Having flown quite a bit in private planes, I know you can lose perspective quite easily.)

Take care?
People who take care
never go anywhere.

Take a chance!

Take charge!

Take control!

"Oh, yes," he said. "I knew I was upside down when I saw the ocean was my sky. Do you know what saved me?"

"What?"

"I was taught that when something terrible happens, don't *do* anything. Just think. So," he said, "that's all I can remember. I did nothing. I never touched a control. If I had not been taught that, I would have instinctively lost the horizontal position I had, and I would have tipped into the water and been killed." He added, "I still remember, when something catastrophic is threatening, *Don't do anything. Just think.*"

12 Don't surrender leadership to the fates.

There are all kinds of negative "fates" that social structures or the "stars" might try to impose upon you. I have been asked under what star I was born. I always reply that I don't know and I don't want to know. Too many people allow their futures to be unnecessarily predetermined by imaginary factors. Astrology is like fortunetelling and I don't like fortunetellers. They make too many negative statements.

I'll never forget this one poor anxiety-prone person who didn't have enough faith in God to go to church. Instead, he went to a fortuneteller, who said, "In your future I see poverty, bad luck, and failure until you reach the age of forty."

To which the person asked, "Then what?"

The fortuneteller looked at him and said, "Oh, after that you get used to it."

Fortunetellers, chart readers, and any others who program people subconsciously or consciously with negative self-fulfilling prophecies are dangerous people. Never allow these people to move into the control position of your life.

13 Don't surrender leadership to forecasts.

You know there are people who are constantly saying, "Things are bad, and they're only going to get worse." There will always be negative, cynical people who only believe that life will go downhill as time goes on.

I love the story the late Bear Bryant, head football coach at the University of Alabama for many years, told me once. Years ago, when he was coach at Texas A&M, his team was scheduled to play SMU in one of the big bowl games. He said, "All of the newspapers said that my team was going to get swamped. These were the words they used: *slaughtered, swamped, driven into the ground.* There was no way I could keep my boys from reading those negative forecasts. So I went to bed the night before the game, and I suddenly remembered all that the reporters and sportscasters were saying: 'Bear Bryant of Texas A&M is going to get beaten by three or four touchdowns.' Others were saying five touchdowns. All of these extremely negative words were in my mind as I fell asleep. I woke up early in the morning. I looked at the clock and it was one o'clock. And I was petrified. We were going to get slaughtered. That was the forecast."

Then he said, "I remembered that Bible verse: 'If you have faith as a grain of mustard seed, you will say to this mountain, "Move from here to there," and it will move; and nothing shall be impossible unto you' [Matt. 17:20]. I got up, called my coaches, and said, 'I want you to have all the players in the locker room in thirty minutes.' I pulled my pants on, put some shoes and a sweater on. I got in the car and started it. The two headlights pierced the blackness of the night. At 1:30 A.M. there wasn't a car on the road. I swung into the parking lot, went into the deserted locker room, paced, and waited. Other car lights started coming, one lonely car after another. The players came staggering in. A couple of them were still in their pajamas and bathrobes.

"I said to them, 'Did you hear the news? Have you heard what they're predicting? They say we're going to get slaughtered. Beaten by four, five, or six touchdowns. You all heard it. O.K. I want to tell you something. Jesus said, "If you have faith as a grain of mustard seed—a little mustard seed—you can say to your mountain, Move! And it will move. And nothing will be impossible to you." Now go home to bed.' "

I asked him, "How did you do?"

He said, "Dr. Schuller, we lost. But by only three points. We lost the game, but boy, we saved our pride!"

14 Don't surrender leadership to your foes.

I had a lot of opposition when I assumed leadership of the construction of the Crystal Cathedral. My opposition did not come from the congregation. They were very supportive in their labor, their love, and their prayers. But from outside the congregation, I had my foes. Their criticisms were hard to take. But through the whole experience I learned this: Not a single opponent, not a single foe, not a single critic offered any better solution to my problem. I soon realized that my foes really weren't interested in solving my problems.

They're not accountable. You and I will stand before God some day, and we will have to give account to Him of what and why we did or did not do certain things. Do you know what hell would be for me? It would be standing before God and having Him look at me and tell me all the things I could have done if I'd had more faith.

This leadership principle might be pretty obvious. What isn't so obvious is the next principle.

15 Don't surrender leadership to your friends.

Every time we have made a decision in this church, one or two of my best friends on the church board couldn't go along with it. Even in my marriage, my wife and I have not always agreed.

Somebody once asked, "How could you be married so successfully for thirty-two years when you don't always agree?" To answer that question I refer to a book my wife has written, *The Positive Family*. In that book she reveals the secret.

We have a scale of nonapproval. When we disagree, we measure the depth of the intensity of nonagreement.

We have a scale from one to ten.

1. The lowest level is, "I'm not enthusiastic. But go ahead if you want to." From there the intensity of the comments increases.

2. "I don't see it the way you do, but I may be wrong, so go ahead."

3. "I don't agree. I'm sure you're wrong. But I can live with it. Go ahead."

4. "I don't agree. But I'll be quiet and let you have your way. I can change it my way later on. Next year I can repaint, repaper, reupholster it my way."

5. "I don't agree, and I cannot remain silent. I love you, but I will not be able to keep from expressing my disapproval. So don't be offended if you hear me expressing a contrary view."

6. "I do not approve, and I make a motion we postpone and delay action until we both are able emotionally and rationally to reevaluate our positions. Give me more time."

7. "I strongly disapprove. This is a mistake—costly, not easily corrected, and I stand firm. I cannot and will not go along with it."

8. "My answer is no! I will be so seriously upset if you go ahead that I cannot predict what my reaction will be."

9. "No way! If you go ahead I have to tell you I quit; I'll walk out!"

10. "No—no—no! Over my dead body!"[3]

I must tell you that in thirty-two years my wife and I have never gone above a six in our level of disagreement.

When I feel myself getting upset, I'll say, "This is a six, Honey." Six means: "I love you very, very much. Since I can't tell what this is going to do to our relationship, which is obviously more important, let's wait and think about it. Maybe in a month or two, I'll be able to approve. However, today I can't agree with you on this. Give me time to see your viewpoint and feel what you feel."

[3]From *The Positive Family*. Copyright © 1982 by Arvella Schuller. Reprinted by permission of Doubleday and Company, Inc.

Friends can give you advice. They can share with you their opinions. But they should never have the final word. The only one who can make the decision and live with the results is you. Do what you believe you must do. Be true to yourself, to your ideals, and to your dreams.

16 Don't surrender leadership to the fracturing experiences of life.

A brokenness can occur that leaves people without faith for the future. A young man said to me after his wife left him for another man, "I'm never going to trust another woman."

I said to him, "Believe in dreams. Never believe in hurts. Don't let your fracturing experience shape your future."

I remember a very dear friend who had a poodle, a lovely, adorable dog. The dog died. I said to her, "Betty, when are you going to get a new puppy?"

She said, "Never again."

I said, "Why not?"

"Oh, it hurts too much to lose them. I'll never have another dog."

I said, "Betty, you can't surrender to a hurt. You can't let the grief and the hurts and the aches and the breaking experiences of life control your future decisions."

17 Don't surrender leadership to the flattening-out experiences of life.

I have seen families in this church that have withstood experiences that would crush others. One of these families was the Van Allen family. Both Ed and Jeanne are now gone, having passed away much too young. Ed Van Allen died when he was transporting a new airplane to a South Pacific mission station. The plane never made Honolulu. No sooner did Ed die than Jeanne got cancer. Jeanne was told that her case was terminal, that she did not have long to live. After courageously fighting a losing battle, she suddenly had a last resurgence. She came back and did some wonderful work and made some fine contributions.

At her deathbed, I asked, "Jeanne, where did you get the power to come back these last few weeks? Three months ago you were almost dead."

She said, "Oh, I began to think, 'This is it. You're terminal. Now's the time to quit, give up.' But then I prayed and this thought came to me: If I give up, two organizations will benefit—the mortuary and the cemetery. But if I hang in there for another month or so, my family will benefit. Maybe my church can benefit.

"So I said to myself, I'm going to get dressed at least once more, and I'm going to work on the telephone—the NEW HOPE Telephone Counseling—at least one day, or at least a couple of hours."

She said, "Then I began to get inspired. I thought of hundreds of things I wanted to do. I just kept saying, 'I'm gonna do this, I'm gonna to do that.' Dr. Schuller, the *'gonnas'* got me going!"

Jeanne didn't give in to the flattening-out experiences. She also practiced the final principle of leadership, the principle that encompasses all of the above.

18 Do surrender leadership to one thing—faith.

Let faith be in control of every decision you make and every action you take. You do that when you let the positive possibilities set your goals.

When you look at your life and where it's headed, ask yourself these questions: "Who's in charge? Who's in control? To whom have I surrendered leadership?"

Surrender leadership to faith. Surrender leadership to God. Let Him be in control of your life. Ask Him three questions: "God, who am I? Why am I here? Where am I headed?" At the very least, His answers may surprise you. They will open your eyes to the beautiful person that you are and will become, as well as to the fantastic future that awaits you.

6

Ten Commandments of Possibility Thinking

Possibility thinking. What is it? In essence it is the management of ideas. Some people never have learned to manage time. Some people never have learned to manage money. Some people never have learned to manage people or themselves. Possibility thinking focuses not on the management of time, money, energy, or persons, but on the management of ideas.

What do we mean by *management*? Management is control. Management is the control of a resource in order to minimize waste and maximize the development of latent possibilities.

I am told that ten thousand ideas daily flow through the average mind. A vast majority of the ideas are negative. Possibility thinking is the disciplined separation of negative thoughts from positive thoughts by this criterion: Positive thoughts are those that hold undeveloped potential for good.

Impossibility thinkers are people who instinctively react negatively to a possibility-laden idea. They impulsively look for reasons why it can't be done. They quickly abort an idea and forget about it.

The possibility thinker looks at every idea to see if it has possibilities. If it does, he takes an option out on the idea. He does not let it slip by.

I recently received a letter from a woman in Flora, Indiana, who was presented with a positive idea, executed it, and is now managing a successful small business. She wrote:

Dear Dr. Schuller:

A few weeks ago I heard you say, "If you are laid off work, you're lucky!" I thought, *Oh, dear, really!* You said, "You probably would not have the guts enough to quit your job and start a business of your own." I thought to myself, *How did you know?*

Well, that is exactly what has happened to me. I was laid off from General Motors in Kokomo, Indiana. I kept busy with my sewing and doing for others, but that didn't pay much. I kept asking God, "If I have a talent, please help me turn it into a business."

In August, my husband and I were helping friends build a cabin in Minnesota, and in evenings we women worked on crafts. My friend said, "I am so tired of making crafts and giving them away, aren't you? Let's start a gift shop with things on consignment." She also said we had the ideal place for the shop—where I used to have my Tupperware office at one end of our garage—a room twenty-four by thirteen feet.

Now this friend had not seen this room since I got out of Tupperware seven years ago. It had become a room for "where do I put this or that? . . . Oh, just out in the Tupperware office." Now, can't you just picture our room like that? When we got back from Minnesota we had fifty names on our list of people we knew who made crafts. We got that messy room cleaned out, had a garage sale, and what didn't sell, the Goodwill got. We got six hundred dollars for stuff we thought was really junk. We thought, *If people will come out in the country for a garage sale, they should come for handmade things.*

So we got very inexpensive pumpkin-colored plaid carpet. We restained the paneling and made curtains with painted pumpkins on the tiebacks and called our place "The Pumpkin Patch Gift Shop." We opened October 1.

In the first month we have had over six hundred people here and have had gross sales of $2,533.22. Before we opened the doors on October 1, we had our long talk with God, and He is our Number One Partner. We now have ninety-four people with lovely handmade things in our place. As we look back, I can't remember any negative thoughts about this. We just feel like it had to be God's idea. We could not have done all this as fast as we have without Him. And we do thank you, Dr. Schuller, for all your help. I talk about you in the Pumpkin Patch lots of times.

This woman is a possibility thinker! She could have rejected her friend's proposal for any number of reasons. Instead, she managed the negative ideas, executed the positive ones, and now her unemployment problem is solved!

I consider myself a possibility thinker. I have pursued many ideas that initially appeared humanly impossible. The results have always amazed me. But, I must confess that there have been many other ideas that were so ludicrous that I quickly rejected them. I never gave them a chance.

Today I was given the keys to a brand-new Lincoln. The car is mine, free of charge, for twelve months. This gift was the result of an impossible dream that I was tempted to discard.

The idea first occurred to me when I was with my wife at the Honolulu airport. We were inquiring about a rental car when the clerk informed us, "We have a super bargain going right now. We have brand-new Lincolns, fully equipped and fully computerized. Normally they rent for sixty dollars a day. We can let you have one for only thirty-five dollars!"

My wife was so enthusiastic she convinced me to rent the car. It was beautiful! It handled like a dream.

That was when I got the idea: "Wouldn't it be great to get a car like this for Arvella [my wife]? After all, she has nearly eighty thousand miles on her old car."

My idea was a good idea. It was a positive idea. It could bring comfort and safety to someone I love. However, when I realized how much a car like that one might cost, I quickly dismissed the thought.

No sooner did I say to myself, *Forget it, Schuller. It's too expensive,* than this next thought came to me: *Why don't you practice what you preach? You just gave a lecture last week at a sales conference. There you told thousands of people how important it is to manage ideas. You said "Never throw away an idea just because it is impossible. Give it a chance."*

So, I decided to give it a try. I thought that I should at least find out what it cost. Maybe it would be less than I imagined. Even if it was as much as I expected, perhaps I could get one on sale. If not, I could try to increase my income somehow. I decided I would try to work it out.

As soon as I made *a sincere commitment to try*, the break-through came! I suddenly recalled meeting a man named Bob Eagle, who was introduced to me as "head of Eagle

Lincoln-Mercury dealership in Dallas, Texas—one of the nation's largest."

Should I call Bob and see if he would sell me one of these cars at cost? The idea seemed crazy. I was tempted once more to discard it. But then I remembered another principle I have lectured on often, "Do it now!"

I walked to the telephone, called the Dallas information operator, and asked for the telephone number of Eagle Lincoln-Mercury. I placed a person-to-person call to Bob Eagle. When the secretary heard it was a person-to-person call from Hawaii, she immediately got Bob on the line. He greeted me warmly.

I relayed to him how impressed I was with this automobile and told him that, though I couldn't afford it, it would be wonderful if I could give one to my wife for her birthday.

Bob said, "Dr. Schuller, you've really helped me through your television show. Now I'd like to help you. Let me see what I can do."

A few minutes later he called back. "There's someone I'd like you to talk to. He's Gordon MacKenzie, vice-president of Ford Motor Company."

Then, by way of a three-way conference call, I met Gordon and accepted an offer to visit the Ford assembly plant later that week when I would be in the Detroit area.

When I arrived in Detroit, I was treated graciously by Gordon and his friend, John Sagan, treasurer of the Ford Motor Company. They took me to dinner and the next morning gave me a personal tour of the assembly plant.

As we were surveying the assembly lines, Gordon MacKenzie said, "Dr. Schuller, I want you to feel free to interrupt any worker on any assembly line and ask him any question you want."

I decided to take him up on his offer and tapped a laborer on the shoulder. MacKenzie introduced me. I said to the worker, "How do you like your job?"

"I love it," he said.

"Why?" I asked.

His eyes flashed and he grinned from ear to ear. Then he

answered, pointing proudly to a beautiful new car: "That's why! I'm so proud to be a part of that car. This is absolutely the greatest automobile made in the world, today. For price and value, it cannot be beat. We have never before produced such an automobile in Detroit! And we know it!"

As I was leaving the plant I turned to MacKenzie and said, "Gordon, I am very impressed by what you're doing here. Nobody could put more quality, care, and dedication into manufacturing a car than you are."

Gordon MacKenzie realized how deeply moved I was at the dedication of the workers in that company, and he said to me, "Dr. Schuller, since you are so impressed we'd like to do something for you. Be our guest and drive one of our cars for the next twelve months—free. And see if everything we are telling you isn't really true!"

That's how I came to be the recipient of keys to a brand-new Lincoln. It never would have happened if I hadn't grabbed hold of my first idea. It makes me wonder how many potential blessings I have carelessly tossed aside because I did not dare to pursue a positive thought.

The point is this: Never underestimate the value of an idea. Every positive idea has within it the potential for success if it is managed properly. How do we manage ideas so effectively that we can be assured of success? Through the Ten Commandments of Possibility Thinking—that's how! If you will obey these commandments for possibility thinking, you will be amazed at the success that you will be able to achieve. What are they?

1 Never reject a possibility because you see something wrong with it!

There is something wrong with every good idea. Any time God gives you an idea, you can find some negative aspect to it. It's amazing how people sit in a deliberating meeting and respond to an opportunity only by finding fault with it. Don't throw away a suggestion when you see a problem. Instead, isolate the negative from the possibility. Neutralize the negative. Exploit the possibility, and sublimate the negative. Don't ever let negatives kill the positive potential that is within an opportunity.

Nothing is impossible if I will hold on to the idea that it might become possible somehow, some way, with someone's help. Only a few weeks ago I was asked to deliver a possibility-thinking seminar for the unemployed. They said, "Dr. Schuller, you believe in possibility thinking. Maybe it can help the unemployed solve their impossible problems and find a job."

Frankly, I was challenged by the idea. It forced me to review the principles of possibility thinking and apply them to an area to which I had never before attempted to apply them.

As I worked on my speech, my notes piled up higher and higher until I realized: *This could be very helpful to a lot of unemployed people. Maybe I should write a book on this subject.*

At that point I could have reacted negatively. Instead, I yielded to that positive impulse, telephoned my publisher and asked, "Could you get a book published, manufactured, and out on the streets of America in a few months? I think I have something to say that could be very helpful to the unemployed. I'd like to get it out in a hurry."

My editor, Larry Stone, said, "I'll call you back."

On Friday the phone rang. It was Larry. "Dr. Schuller, we love the slogan 'Tough times never last . . . but tough people do!' We'd love to have you write a book with that title. It could be very, very helpful to many people. And we agree that it must get out in a hurry. A lot of people are desperate and need that hope today.

"Our spring catalog goes to print in three days. If you're agreeable, we'll announce your new book in the spring catalog. It will say that your book will be coming out in six months. O.K.?"

I was excited. "You bet!" I answered.

Then he dropped the bombshell, "If we are to deliver what we are promising, we will need the first four chapters from you by November 15."

"No problem," I answered impulsively. "You'll have it!"

*Better to
do something
imperfectly
than to
do nothing
flawlessly.*

My wife had heard the conversation and said, "What have you agreed to do?" I explained. She said, "Do you know what date it is today?"

I said, "No."

"The fifteenth of November is a week from Monday."

I was horrified. "A week from Monday? There is no way I can get four chapters by that time! Tomorrow is Saturday and I'll need all day Saturday to write the two Sunday morning messages I am scheduled to deliver."

The only free day I had before November 15 was Monday, the eighth. How could I possibly get four chapters written before the fourteenth of November? I concluded inwardly that I had agreed to the impossible. Yet everything within me refused to give up on the idea. Somehow it would have to be accomplished.

On Monday morning I was not at all motivated. In fact, I was paralyzed by anxiety.

I allowed myself to be interrupted by telephone calls. I allowed myself to be distracted by other pressures.

By the time I went to bed at 10:30 on Monday night I had not lifted a pen. I had not written a thing on my book. That meant that I now had only six days left to write four chapters.

You are reading the book, so you can see that I got the chapters done in time. What saved me? Was it a positive slogan? Prodding from my wife? No. It was an obscene phone call.

On Tuesday morning, November 9, 1982, the phone awakened me at 4:30. The person on the other end never said a word. There was just some heavy breathing.

I turned over, hoping to catch another couple hours of rest, but was unable to go back to sleep. As I tossed and turned, this thought occurred to me: *Why don't you get up? Go into the library and start dictating.* But I argued with myself: *I can't dictate a book. I never dictate books! That is something in which I've never believed.* (Don't ask me why. It only illustrates my problem of locked-in thinking on a particular point.)

But then I remembered that I am supposed to be a possibility thinker. *Schuller, practice what you preach. Anything is possible. Maybe it is also possible to dictate a book. At least it will help you to get started. Remember what you wrote in* Move Ahead with Possibility Thinking: *"Beginning is half done."*

That did it. I responded to the idea. I slipped out of bed, walked to the library, and dictated in the silent darkness of the early morning. I spoke without interruption for two hours. By this time the darkness had turned to dawning. The sun was rising. My daughters were stirring in their bedrooms. The day was just beginning, but I had already written one complete chapter.

The rest of my day was full. There was no other time for writing. But I went to bed that night confident that one chapter was finished. At three o'clock on Wednesday morning I was awakened by our dogs. Our Samoyed, Doberman, and German Shepherd would not quit barking. Finally I got out of bed to quiet them down and discovered that they had cornered a raccoon under our front porch. They were barking with insane rage at this cowering, cornered creature. I tried to bribe the dogs with food to quiet them. I commanded them to be quiet. Nothing worked.

I was disgusted. I went back to bed. I couldn't get to sleep. So for the second morning in a row I went to my library and dictated another chapter for the book.

Then I called my senior editor, who edits my sermons every Sunday and consequently knows all of my material better than anybody else! That person is my daughter, Sheila Schuller Coleman. I said, "Sheila, I need to get two more chapters written in the next few days. Remember the story of Birt, Benno, and John, our NEW HOPE counselor who was paralyzed? Would you pull them together into a chapter? And would you help me polish up the other chapters that I have dictated? Could you take my lecture on the Ten Commandments for Possibility Thinkers and develop it into a fourth chapter?

"Sure, Dad!" she replied enthusiastically.

The story that I am sharing with you now, I dictated on Thursday morning at 4:30! A few hours later I left for Arizona, then Indiana. I arrived back in town late Friday night. On Saturday, I prepared two messages for Sunday. But on my desk Saturday morning were the four completed chapters of this new book, *Tough Times Never Last, But Tough People Do!*

What I would have considered to be a total impossibility became an accomplished fact!

2 Never reject a possibility because you won't get the credit!

God can do tremendous things through the person who doesn't care who gets the credit. Years ago, I met a man who was president and chairman of the board of a company in Minneapolis. The company had made the first huge balloon satellite, one that moved across the night sky like a star. It was a successful step in the early stages of the space program. I said to the president, "Excuse me for saying this, but I've never heard of your name or your company."

He replied, "Maybe not. We didn't get the credit, but we got the contract."

Don't worry about getting the credit. If you do, you'll become ego-involved in the decision-making moments of life. Decisions must never be based on ego needs. They must be based on human needs and market pressures that transcend your own desires. Decide today: Would you rather satisfy your ego—or enjoy the fruit of success?

3 Never reject an idea because it's impossible!

Almost every great idea is impossible when it is first born. The greatest ideas today are yet impossible! Possibility thinkers take great ideas and turn the impossibilities into possibilities. That's progress!

The important issue is whether the idea is a good one. Would it help people who are hurting? Would it be a great

*When faced
with a mountain,
I will not quit!
I will
keep on striving
until I climb over,
find a pass through,
tunnel underneath—
or simply stay
and turn the mountain
into a gold mine,
with God's help!*

thing for our country and our world? If so, then develop a way to achieve what today is impossible.

Not many days ago I was in Singapore, talking with a Nobel Prize-winning biologist who's active in genetic engineering and the forefront of gene-splicing. He predicts that if given freedom to do so, geneticists will be able to develop a plant agriculturally designed to generate an alcoholic fuel that will produce maximum mileage for sophisticated engines not yet conceived. That's possibility thinking! Just because it's impossible today doesn't mean it will be impossible tomorrow. Our goals should always be based upon whether it would be a sensational thing to accomplish.

4 Never reject a possibility because your mind is already made up!

I'm sure you've heard the saying: "Don't confuse me with the facts, my mind is already made up!" I've had to change my mind publicly more than once. People who never change their minds are either perfect or stubborn. I'm not perfect and neither are you. I'd rather change plans while still in port, than to set sail and sink at sea.

5 Never reject an idea because it's illegal!

Listen carefully, or you'll misinterpret this commandment. Some of the greatest ideas are impossible because they are illegal today. You should never violate the law, but don't reject an idea because it's illegal. You might be able to get the law changed!

A good friend of mine, Bill Brashears, acquired fourteen property lots to develop a twelve-acre commercial center. But he ran into a major problem. There was a flood control channel through the middle of his property, and it was illegal to erect a building over a flood control channel. That could have killed the project for him, but I gave him this advice: "Never reject an idea because it's illegal. The law is inadequate—so get it changed. After all, they built the Prudential Building in Chicago over the railroad tracks. Why can't we have a little water go under a building in Orange County?" So Bill led a crusade, and the law was changed. A lot of laws on the books today need to be changed.

6 Never reject an idea because you don't have the money, manpower, muscle, or months to achieve it!

All it takes to accomplish the impossible is mind power, manpower, money power, muscle power, and month power. If you don't have them, you can get them. Spend enough time, use enough energy, develop enough human resources, acquire enough financial capital, and you can do almost anything. Don't reject an idea just because you don't have the necessary power. Make the commitment to do what's great, then solve the problems. A supersuccessful person has very few resources, except the capacity to take an idea and marshal stronger and smarter people around him to pull it off.

Many years ago, when the beautiful Union Railroad Station was built in Cincinnati, Ohio, spectacular mosaics were created on the plastered walls. They artfully depicted the crafts and industry of the city of Cincinnati.

As years went by, the building began to sag. When it was condemned, people were horrified. What would happen to the exquisite mosaics? Destroying them along with the building was unthinkable.

Yet, when the experts were consulted, they replied, "There is no way to save the mosaics when the building is destroyed."

Alfred Moore refused to accept that answer. He could not let the mosaics be destroyed. He decided that he would find a way. That decision was the key that unlocked his mind. He thought of one possible way the twenty-by-twenty-foot panels could be moved.

He created a gigantic steel frame for the section of the wall. Then he put wire nets on the back side of the wall, and sprayed it with gunnite—the wet concrete that is used in swimming pools. Then, with a huge crane, he lifted the walls, transported them, and installed them in the new airport. They are there today!

7 Never reject an idea because it will create conflict!

The longer I've studied possibility thinking, the more I've come to one conclusion. You can never develop a possibility without creating problems. You can never establish a goal without generating a new set of tensions. You can never make a commitment without producing some conflict. Every idea worth anything is bound to be rejected by people who don't go along with it. To reject an idea because it may generate conflict is to "surrender leadership" to friends or foes!

8 Never reject an idea because it's not your way of doing things!

Learn to accommodate. Prepare to compromise. Plan to adjust. A different style, a new policy, a change in tradition—all are opportunities to grow. Get set to compromise. Learn to be equilibristic. Maintain a balance between the tension of an opportunity that demands exploitation and the limitations of the resources available at the moment. Readjust your budget. Compromise your taste. Accommodate your life-style. You may have to decide, "It's more important to succeed than it is to snobbishly adhere to my private tastes."

9 Never reject an idea because it might fail!

Every idea worth anything has failure potential within it. There is risk in everything. One thing the United States needs more than anything today is possibility thinking.

I've recently returned from a trip to Singapore, where they have an impressive amount of productivity. Singapore imports 100 percent of its oil, and it's not getting any discounts. If Singapore pays the same price we're paying, and it has to import everything, why is it so successful? The people there are better at possibility thinking.

Our problem in this country is with management, labor, and consumers. Consumers are told that if there is anything wrong with a product, don't buy it, and if you do buy it, sue the company. Labor has its problems. Management has its problems. I don't think there is anything worse than the no-risk mentality we have in America.

If Jesus Christ had operated that way, He would never have died on the cross. The whole principle of faith means you're prepared to make a supreme sacrifice for the greater good of other persons. There can be no assurance until that happens. Success is never certain, and failure is never final.

People look at my ministry and think it is a success. It is. But for how long? By the grace of God, *only as long as we can make it so.* Success is never carved in granite. It is always molded in clay. America thought it had it made, but now we're being surpassed. We were so successful before that, while we took long lunch breaks, others were running on ahead of us.

You never reject an idea because there's some risk involved. You isolate the risk, insulate it, and eventually eliminate it.

10 Never reject an idea because it's sure to succeed!

There are people today who back off if they are sure they will succeed. One reason is that these persons begin to imagine the ego fulfillment this success would give, and with an excuse of being humble, they pull out.

To all of my fellow Christians, trying to follow Jesus, who say, "I should not try to be successful. I'm not trying for the top of the ladder. That's vanity. That's materialistic," I must say, that's not true! To choose poverty instead of prosperity, failure instead of success, low achievement instead of top-of-the-ladder achievement, simply for the sake of being humble, is not super-Christian. It's dumb. Only successful people can help people who are failing. Only winners will survive to give food to the hungry.

Rich DeVos, a member of our board and president of Amway Corporation, has a favorite saying: "The poor cannot help the poor." Because an idea gives you ego-fulfillment does not mean it is not coming from God. Philippians 2:13 puts it very bluntly: "It is God who works in you both to will and to do for His good pleasure." Just because an idea is going to be a success, don't be against it.

The Ten Commandments for Possibility Thinkers—where do I get them? All ten come from the Bible. All ten come from Jesus Christ—the World's Greatest Possibility Thinker. He said, "If you have faith as a mustard seed, you will say to this mountain, 'Move from here to there,' and it will move; and nothing will be impossible for you" (Matt. 17:20).

7

Count to Ten and Win!

Many years ago I discovered a formula for solving insolvable problems. It's a formula that has never failed me. I call it "Playing the Possibility Thinking Game." I referred to it in *You Can Become the Person You Want to Be*, but here I will show you how it can help you manage your problems and overcome difficulties.

I discovered the exercise in creative thinking quite accidentally—or was it providentially?

The year was 1955. I had accepted an invitation to come to California to begin a new church. I was told that the sponsoring denomination would finance the purchase of two acres of land at the cost of four thousand dollars. In addition, I was given five hundred dollars. That was it. I was expected to come up with my own financing for the first little building. After it was built, I could start holding services and hopefully collect a nucleus of charter members. I suggested that I could start holding services in some empty hall while we were putting the financial package together and designing the first simple little chapel. "There isn't an empty hall around the town," my advisor replied. "It's impossible to find an empty hall or an empty building in Garden Grove!"

Such were the premises when I packed my family into our '53 Chevrolet to drive from Chicago to California.

I was in a café in Albuquerque, New Mexico, with my wife, my six-month-old baby boy, Robert Anthony, and my four-year-old daughter Sheila. My mind was wandering, racing ahead to my California destination, now only two days away.

"There must be an empty hall somewhere in that town!" I blurted out to my wife, sitting across the table.

Then I did something quite intuitively and impulsively. I picked up the paper napkin, and on the back side I wrote the numerals "1" to "10" vertically on the left side of the paper. I let my imagination run wild. My list looked like this:

1. Rent a school building.
2. Rent a Masonic Hall.
3. Rent an Elk's Lodge.
4. Rent a mortuary chapel.
5. Rent an empty warehouse.
6. Rent a community club building.
7. Rent a Seventh-Day Adventist Church.
8. Rent a Jewish synagogue.
9. Rent a drive-in theater.
10. Rent an empty piece of ground, a tent, and folding chairs.

Suddenly what had seemed totally impossible now seemed possible. Suddenly the word *impossible* sounded irresponsible, extreme, reactionary, and unintelligent.

This list was my first rudimentary effort in playing a game that I would play many times in the next thirty years.

I had made my list. I then proceeded to check out each of my possibilities. Possibility number one was scratched when I discovered that it was against the law to rent a school building. (That law has since been changed.)There was no Masonic Hall or Elk's Lodge in Garden Grove. The Baptists were already meeting in the only mortuary chapel in town. The Presbyterians were renting the Seventh-Day Adventist Church on Sunday. There was no Jewish synagogue. I couldn't find an empty warehouse or an empty community club building.

I was down to possibility number nine. There was a drive-in theater on the outskirts of the city. *Too far away from the center of Garden Grove*, I thought to myself. But after that negative thought, a positive thought entered my mind. And the positive thought was, *It may not be in the center of Garden Grove, but it is in the center of Orange County!* The rest is history. I went to the drive-in theater. I was told it was available at ten dollars a Sunday! And it had parking for seventeen hundred cars.

I started preaching in that drive-in theater four weeks later. I eventually spent six years preaching under the open sky without protection from the winter rains, insects, or birds.

Years later, we erected our first building. In ten years, the church grew to a membership of fifteen hundred persons. We now needed offices and counseling quarters to minister to the expanded needs of the hurting people in our community. We calculated that all of the offices needed for counselors and ministers would occupy too much ground space. Then I thought, *Why not build it in a high-rise tower?* After all, a tower could be a landmark, pointing out the location of the church to passersby on neighboring roads. The church steeple is respected and traditional on the landscapes of western Europe and the United States of America.

Why not build a church tower, a steeple, that would not only have height—but would also be functional from the top to the bottom? Why not put a couple of elevators in the tower, divide it into floors, put a chapel at the top and fill it with offices and counseling facilities?

It was an exciting idea. But again I had absolutely no money. But to play the possibility thinking game, you have to assume that *you won't win if you don't begin*. There's no hope of winning if you don't decide to play the game.

I decided to *win*. And to win, I needed to *begin*. I went to the bank in Garden Grove and opened a special "Tower of Hope" fund. In it I deposited twenty-five dollars. Then I went before the congregation and shared, in a message that I hoped would be inspiring, my dream of a counseling center that could minister to people in the community and across the nation. I shared with them a vision of installing telephones in the tower to receive calls from desperate people all over the United States. The phone number would be one that anybody would remember—the letters *N-E-W H-O-P-E*.

You won't win
if you don't begin!

In addition, I imagined that we'd have a chapel at the top of the tower, where young people could be married. They could look out to the left and see Catalina Island lying in the Pacific Ocean. They could look to the north and see the snow-capped mountains. They could look around the county and see the freeways and the highways twinkling with the lights of moving traffic and believe they could rise above human problems.

This was the picture I painted for my congregation. This was my dream of a Tower of Hope. "It will cost a million dollars," I told them. "We have twenty-five dollars from an anonymous donor. All we need is another $999,975, and up it goes!"

A couple of people came up to me afterwards and said, "It was a great sermon, Dr. Schuller. And it's a great idea. But it will take a lot of money. I don't know where you're going to get it."

That week I received a letter commending me on the idea and enclosing a check of five hundred dollars. With such an enthusiastic endorsement, I immediately went to the architect, Richard Neutra. I said, "I have an idea for a functional church tower." I sketched out my dream for him—a chapel at the top, counseling offices on the lower floors. "Now, Mr. Neutra," I asked, "I need a pretty picture of this tower."

I handed him my rough black-and-white pencil sketches and said, "Can you make it look pretty? Give it your style? And can you do it in color? And can you do it for $525?"

He smiled at me and said, "I shouldn't agree to it. But I will!" Before I knew it, the picture was delivered. It was a beautiful four-color rendering.

I posted it in the lobby of the church with the announcement: *"This* is what we are going to build!"

The poster inspired a few small gifts. In addition, I published my first book about that time and earmarked my royalties for this project. That boosted the total to six thousand dollars. That six thousand dollars began earning 6 percent interest and was compounding.

I calculated that if we never received another single contribution, that the six thousand dollars would grow into one million dollars in about one hundred years. I told the entire congregation, "If any of you think that the Tower of Hope will never be built, you're wrong! It's going to be built. We already have a million dollars. The only problem is, we can't collect it until one hundred years have passed!" They laughed. I laughed. The important thing was that the project was taken more seriously. We still needed to generate more momentum; however, I needed an idea to lift the project from its launching pad.

At that point I again picked up a piece of paper. I played the possibility thinking game. At the top of the paper I wrote "*$1,000,000.*"

1. Get 1 person to give $1,000,000.
2. Get 2 people to give $500,000.
3. Get 4 people to give $250,000.
4. Get 10 people to give $100,000.
5. Get 20 people to give $50,000.
6. Get 40 people to give $25,000.
7. Get 50 people to give $20,000.
8. Get 100 people to give $10,000.
9. Get 200 people to give $5,000.
10. Get 1,000 people to give $1,000.

I took a look at the list of ten possible ways to get one million dollars, and unknown to me, I'd already cracked an impossibly hard nut. I had listed ten *possible* ways to do what was *impossible* at that moment.

I never did believe I could get a one-million-dollar gift from a single individual. Consequently, I never tried possibility number one.

I did hire a professional fund-raiser to help me organize a campaign. "We'll ask one person to give a hundred thousand dollars, and we'll have other contributions in varying brackets, fifty thousand, twenty-five thousand, and ten thousand dollars," I told my organizer.

"Do you know of anybody who could give one hundred thousand dollars?" he asked.

I said, "I really don't." But then I thought, *Well, there is probably one family that could give ten thousand dollars a year. In ten years that would add up to one hundred thousand dollars*. I was willing to wait ten years for the building. As soon as I thought in those longer terms of years, my problem became manageable and solvable!

We launched the campaign. We called on all of the members of the church. One family, the Vernon Dragts, pledged the hundred thousand dollars over a ten-year period. Actually, they paid it long before that time was up!

When we announced we had a pledge of one hundred thousand dollars, we stimulated enough momentum that the congregation began to believe that this idea was not only possible, it was highly *probable*! That's when I learned that people want to join an exciting, adventuresome, and challenging idea that looks like it will succeed.

The Tower of Hope was built! We borrowed more than eight hundred thousand dollars, aiming to repay it through pledges over the next ten years. In 1968 the tower was opened and stands today as a magnificent landmark in California.

An impossibility became a possibility as soon as I began to play the possibility thinking game. More than any other exercise that I have used, it has stimulated the creative solution to an impossible problem.

I have used it often because each time I solved one problem I found I was faced with another. Twenty years after I had started the church that God called me to build, I had successfully solved countless problems. The tower was built, and the television ministry was launched and financially self-supporting.

But now we faced a new problem. We had outgrown our sanctuary. We needed a larger building. Because of the six years of worshiping in a drive-in theater, I found myself now driven by a deep compulsion to order a structure that would give me an uncluttered view of the sky.

Six years in the drive-in theater revived my country childhood love of the sky and its impact on the worshiping soul.

Without those years I *never* would have been deeply shaped to desire an all-glass building. The comments I made to the architect, Philip Johnson, were, "I really don't want a building. I want to worship in a garden. God's idea of a church was the Garden of Eden."

When Philip Johnson delivered a six-inch plastic model of what would eventually be called the Crystal Cathedral, I fell in love with the concept. But I shuddered at the thought of what it might cost.

After all, I had not given him any limitations when it came to the budget. (I had decided to live by the principle that I had taught: "Nobody has a money problem—only an idea problem.") When he had asked me what kind of budget restrictions he would have to keep in mind, I replied, "Mr. Johnson, we can't afford a million-dollar building, we can't afford a two- or three-million-dollar building, we can't afford a four-million-dollar building. We can't afford anything! Therefore, it doesn't make any difference what it costs!

"The important thing is that the building should generate enough excitement that it will in itself attract the money."

Unhampered by budget restrictions, Philip Johnson unveiled this absolutely spectacular design. On my desk rested the model of what I believed would be one of the great architectural structures of the centuries. "What will it cost?" I asked the architect.

"I think you can build it for seven million dollars," he replied. I gulped. I didn't reveal what I was thinking: *Seven million! So much money!* It was far more than I could handle. It emotionally defeated me for a moment. Our cash flow could not handle such an increase. We would have to raise the money in cold, hard, unborrowed cash. Seven million dollars was a bigger figure than I could comprehend.

When an all-consuming dream fills the human mind with an all-consuming desire, only to be followed by the harsh reality that the entire concept is impossible—then the emotional spectrum moves from an all-time high to an all-time low. Excitement and peak enthusiasm give way to severe discouragement and depression. That was my experience.

I turned to my book *You Can Become the Person You Want to Be* and read the chapter that outlined the possibility thinking game. Once again I took a piece of paper and wrote "$7,000,000" at the top. I wrote "1" to "10" vertically. I prayed intensively. I totally committed the impossible dream to the God whom I believed inspired the dream. I opened my mind to ideas and soon found myself facing ten possible ways to do what I knew was impossible.

1. Get 1 gift of $7,000,000.
2. Get 7 gifts of $1,000,000.
3. Get 14 gifts of $500,000.
4. Get 28 gifts of $250,000.
5. Get 70 gifts of $100,000.
6. Get 100 gifts of $70,000.
7. Get 140 gifts of $50,000.
8. Get 280 gifts of $25,000.
9. Sell each window—10,866 windows—at $500 per window—$5,000,000 plus.

That was as far as I got. I was already enthusiastic. I believed that the project was possible where only minutes before it was a total impossibility. I'd cracked the hardest nut I was ever asked to crack in my life!

I never did ask any person to give seven million dollars. Why not? Because I doubted I could have maintained my own freedom. I was afraid I could have been intimidated by any person that would donate such a large sum of money to the Cathedral! I would be tempted to become a slave as some politicians have to some single, powerful, financial source.

I did move to the second possibility, although I could not comprehend anyone making a gift of one million dollars. I belong to a denomination that is the oldest Protestant denomination with an unbroken ministry in the United States of America—The Reformed Church in America. Fifty-four Dutch colonists, all members of the Reformed Church in the Netherlands, bought Manhattan Island in 1628, built a Dutch windmill, and held worship services in the loft. That church continues today. It is the well-known Marble Collegiate

Church in New York City. In more than three hundred years our denomination has never received a single gift of one million dollars from a living donor.

Again I prayed and recalled reading how one person had contributed a million dollars to a southern California YMCA building many years before. I made contact with the donor. He agreed to see me. I shared with him the blueprints and the model of the Crystal Cathedral. He was fascinated by it. I said to him, "It'll never get built until people take it seriously and believe in it. They won't believe in it unless we get a major gift. Would you, could you, make a lead-off gift of one million dollars?" I will never forget the immediate look in his eyes. It was one of sadness.

"I'd like to, but I can't."

I wasn't surprised. It was a long shot on my part. After all, we didn't know each other.

"May I pray before I leave?" I asked.

"Of course," he said.

I found myself praying, "Dear God, was it Your idea or was it my idea to build this Crystal Cathedral?" and I waited. I wanted to hear His answer deep down in my heart. I asked a second question, "Dear God, was it Your idea that I ask this man to give one million dollars? Or was it my idea?" And I waited long for the reply. Then I continued, "Dear God, I'm so thankful that he said he wants to do it and would like to give it. But he has also said he cannot. Is it possible for You, Father, to figure out a way for him to do what he would like to do?" I waited. Long. Silently. Then I closed the prayer with "Thank You, Father, for listening. Amen."

The next morning at 11:07, the telephone rang in my study. It was the donor. "Dr. Schuller, that building has got to be built. You're right. It'll never be built until people believe it. People won't believe it until there is a major gift. I don't know how, and I don't know when, but I'll give the first gift of one million dollars." I screamed with delight.

It was possibly the single most ecstatic moment in my life. Within sixty days he delivered fifty-five thousand shares of his company's stock at a value of over $18 a share. When sold, it netted $987,000 cash in our special savings account! We were on our way!

I quickly moved on to another possibility in the list of ten possibilities. We announced the sale of windows at $500 per window. Within six months, we successfully sold ten thousand windows. Most of them were being purchased at $25 a month for a twenty-month payment plan.

The project moved from an impossibility to a possibility simply through the possibility thinking game!

I wouldn't want to leave you with the impression that it was all that easy. When it looked as though the cash would be readily available through the above strategies, we made a calculated decision to increase the cost of the building from seven million to ten million dollars by building an entire structure underneath the floor of the Cathedral. This additional structure would provide offices for the entire music department and television production department.

I looked once more over the list of ten ways to raise money. I decided to give possibility number two another try. I approached a donor in Chicago, Illinois, who promised, "I'll give you the tenth million when you have nine million dollars raised in cash." Success looked easy and certain. But then we were hit with inflation, which boosted the price beyond the expected price of ten million to more than fourteen million dollars! That did not include the architectural or engineering fees which would be 8 percent of the construction cost—an additional one million dollars. That was not all. This did not include furnishings and special electronic equipment, which would boost the price by yet another two million!

What was anticipated as a ten-million-dollar project now looked closer to seventeen million! If I were to be totally honest with you, I'd have to say that those were the darkest days of my life. Four months had passed since we had collected our first million dollars. By this time we had spent almost two million in architectural fees, engineering costs, and other beginning expenses.

I called my key persons and offered to abort the project. "You can't do that," I was told. "Your integrity is at stake.

Don't kill
the dream—
execute it!

People want their names on windows. We promised it to them. You have to follow through. Think bigger! And don't contemplate anything less than the fulfillment of the God-given dream."

I followed that advice. We prayed. We dug the hole. We started construction. The bank offered a loan of three and a half million dollars. That was surely not enough. But added to the money we were raising, it was a boost.

We launched another major fund-raising drive to try to collect another million dollars on a single Sunday. I had used an inheritance check of ten thousand dollars some years before to purchase an ocean-front condominium for thirty-eight thousand dollars. I found that it had escalated in value to one hundred seventy-five thousand dollars. I contributed it to the million-dollar Sunday. The momentum was established and the million-dollar Sunday offering was a success!

Two months later an unsolicited offer from a total stranger in Chicago, Illinois, came to me in the form of a letter that said in essence, "I've seen pictures of your proposed Crystal Cathedral. I think it is very exciting. What's the financial status to date? Would an extra million dollars from an old gentleman in Chicago be helpful?" I flew to Chicago and met with him and his wife.

"When do you need the money?" he said. "Actually," I reported, "we are building the building on a pay-as-we-go basis. We will have exhausted our cash and are being told by our contractor Clair Peck that he will stop construction if we have not put another million dollars into the escrow account within thirty days."

The gentleman looked across the room at his wife and said, "Well, Mary, I think we can give Dr. Schuller a million dollars within the next thirty days, don't you?"

Within thirty days, a cashier's check in that amount was delivered!

Two months later he invited me back to Chicago to celebrate his birthday at a very small and intimate gathering in the country club on the North Shore. As I left the dinner party, he handed me an envelope and said, "Dr. Schuller, I want to be selfish on my birthday and give myself a lot of fun. Here is a letter that I've written very selfishly to give myself a great deal of joy. Read it in the car, and you'll understand."

I got in the car and opened the envelope. There was a simple little note that said in effect, "I find my greatest joy in giving gifts to people and projects I love." And with the note was another million-dollar cashier's check for the Crystal Cathedral—our fourth million-dollar commitment!

Construction continued without abatement. And in September 1980, the building was completed. The final cost was nearly twenty million dollars. The only mortgage was a three-and-a-half-million-dollar, ten-year, 9½ percent bank loan against pledges outstanding that would all be collected in another twenty-four months. We could say the building was dedicated "debt-free."

The entire project was successful, all because I was able to count to ten!

Anyone can count to ten—and anyone can be a success! It's true. Count to ten and win. This simple possibility thinking game can help anyone with any problem. I even shared it with the city leaders of Flint, Michigan.

When I was leading the unemployment seminar there, included on my schedule was a noontime luncheon with five hundred city leaders. I knew there were twenty-five thousand people unemployed. So I suggested that the city really needed to create twenty-five thousand new jobs. "And if you think that's impossible," I challenged them, "let's count to ten and believe that we can win." At the top of the blackboard I wrote "25,000 Jobs." Below I listed vertically ten possible ways to create twenty-five thousand new jobs.

1. Get 1 company to move into Flint and produce 25,000 new jobs.
2. Get 2 companies to move in, each providing 12,500 jobs.
3. Get 5 companies to hire 5,000 people each.

4. Get 10 companies to hire 2,500 people each.
5. Get 50 companies to provide 500 new jobs each.
6. Get 100 companies to provide 250 new jobs each.
7. Get 200 companies to provide 125 new jobs each.
8. Get 250 companies to provide 100 new jobs each.
9. Get 500 companies to provide 50 new jobs each.
10. Get 1,000 companies to provide 25 new jobs each.

We were thinking constructively. We had many possibilities that, moments before, hadn't been there.

I challenged the civic leaders. "How can you possibly find these companies?" Answering my own question, I suggested, "Try using the '1 to 10' technique with each of the above possibilities. First, make a list of ten companies *in the world* that could possibly be persuaded to move to Flint, Michigan, and produce twenty-five thousand new jobs." Seeing the look of hope in their eyes, I continued, "But I hope you don't succeed! Why? Because any city that is dependent on one single industry for twenty-five thousand new jobs is too vulnerable! A much better solution would be to find several companies that will create new jobs.

"Go to the existing companies and challenge them to expand their markets and increase their sales productivity to the point that they'll need to hire more people. Look at all of the possible job-producing forces in this world. Consider the federal government. Perhaps it could be motivated to create new jobs in this town. Consider the state and county governments. Consider overseas operations. Look at the companies in Germany, Japan, and Korea that might be persuaded with incentives to come to Flint, Michigan!"

I wish I could report, as of this writing, that the above "count to ten and win" technique had produced twenty-five thousand new jobs in Flint. I cannot report that. But I can report that hundreds of new jobs have been created. And beginning is half the battle!

I have no doubt that if a power committee were established to pursue all of the possibilities that the city could actually create twenty-five thousand new jobs! It might take five years to do it. It might take ten years to do it. It might be accomplished in two or three years. But it's possible!

But you say, your problem is not financial? Maybe it isn't. And maybe it is!

Let me ask this question: "If I were to give you a million dollars in cash, do you think you could solve the problems you are facing today?"

Think about it for a day or two. Think about it for a week. And if the answer could conceivably be yes, then go after a million dollars!

Count to ten and win. Why does it work? What are the dynamics that cause it to be so effective? I said it in *You Can Become the Person You Want to Be*, "Consider the mind set that results from 'game attitude.'" When you adopt the attitude that it's only a game, emotionally you are free. What are the attitudes characteristic of someone who is playing a game? They are:

1. Risk-running: The fear of failure is absent. "If I lose, it's only a game." You dare to think in almost reckless dimensions. This is the arena in which progress is always made.
2. Record-breaking: This mental attitude causes you to think bigger, reach farther, try harder, than you ever have before. You are putting yourself in a frame of mind where you can think bigger than you have ever thought before. Almost always the inventive solution to every problem is that simple. Spend more money. Hire more people. Form a new organization. Travel farther. Telephone an expert in Europe, etc.
3. Commitment-freeing: Since it's only a game, you can quit any time you want without ruining your reputation. You are free from the subconscious tension generated by the fear of involvement and ongoing responsibilities. Because it's only a game, you can relax in total freedom from responsibility.

When you adopt such game-playing attitudes you generate a mental climate conducive to creativity. This is the secret behind the possibility-thinking game, "Count to Ten and Win."

The word *possibility* is another key to the success of this formula. The very word *possibility* creates a mental climate conducive to creativity. Simply suggesting that something might be possible releases creative brain cells from their invisible prison of subconscious defense mechanisms.

To understand the cybernetic power of this word, consider its antonym, that dirty thirteen-letter word *impossibility*. When uttered aloud, this word is devastating in its effect. Thinking stops. Progress is halted. Doors slam shut. Research comes to a screeching halt. Further experimentation is torpedoed. Projects are abandoned. Dreams are discarded. The brightest and the best of the creative brain cells nosedive, clam up, hide out, cool down, and turn off in some dark, subterranean corner of the mind. In this defensive maneuver, the brain shelters itself against the painful sting of insulting disappointments, brutal rejections, and dashed hopes.

But, let someone utter the magic words *It's possible*. Those stirring words, with the siren appeal of a marshaling trumpet, penetrate into the subconscious tributaries of the mind, challenging and calling those proud powers to turn on and turn out new ideas! Buried dreams are resurrected. Sparks of fresh enthusiasm flicker, then burst into new flame. Tabled motions are brought back to the floor. Dusty files are reopened. Lights go on again in the darkened laboratories. Telephones start ringing. Typewriters make clattering music. Budgets are revised and adopted. "Help wanted" signs are hung out. Factories are retooled and reopened. New products appear. New markets open. The recession has ended. A great new era of adventure, experimentation, expansion, and prosperity is born.

Now you too can play the possibility thinking game. Here's how:

Rule number one: Begin by believing that you possess latent gifts of creativity. You will respect, trust, and admire your own thoughts. *Every* person can be creative.

Rule number two: Don't play it alone. Play it with problem-solving people. Play it with possibility-thinking people. Play it with people who have a record of achievement and success. You *can* play it alone. But a lot of ideas might come from others.

All it takes is one idea to solve an impossible problem! It might be one of those ideas that you will write down on the piece of paper. Or it could be a combination of several of the ideas that are put down on the paper.

Remember this. You won't start winning without a beginning.

8

The Faith That Can Move Your Mountain

So you've tried to believe, and still you're unemployed? You think you've applied faith to your problem, and it still won't go away? You've exercised all the faith you can muster, and difficulties still abound?

Someone once said to me: "Was Jesus wrong? Did He make a mistake when He said, 'If you have faith as a mustard seed, you will say to this mountain, 'Move from here to there,' and it will move; and nothing shall be impossible for you' [Matt. 17:20]?" My answer is one that can give you the inner toughness to see your tough time through until light breaks around you.

Faith is indeed the greatest miracle-working power imaginable. Faith never fails a person; we fail when we give up on our faith. However, if we cut out any one of the five phases of faith, we will be disappointed with the ultimate results.

Faith is like a seed. If a seed is not planted, it can't bear fruit. But planting is just the first phase. Unless the seed is watered, it won't sprout. Sprouting is the second phase. Once the seed is planted and watered, growth will begin. But unless the plant is nourished, it will not reach full maturity. It will not blossom, which is the third phase.

Then when the buds are beginning to form, if the proper climatic conditions do not exist, the stalk will produce no fruit. There will be no ear on the corn. Bearing fruit is the fourth phase of the cycle. Only if each phase is properly nurtured can a seed reach full maturity. Finally, when the fruit is ripe, it must be harvested at the precisely correct time, or winds, rain, or overripeness can cause it to drop to the ground, where it will rot. Even as there are five phases to fruit-bearing, from the planting of the seed to harvest there are five phases to the full cycle of mountain-moving faith.

The Nesting Phase

The first phase of faith is the nesting phase. That's when an idea drops into the mind as an egg is deposited in the bird's nest. Some people experience only this first phase of faith. For too many people, faith never gets beyond the nesting phase. The unhatched egg rots in the nest. The idea passes through the mind without being taken seriously.

I don't think anything kills the potential miracle-working power of faith more than a lack of self-confidence. Faith is indeed most fragile at birth.

The thought of picking up a new career in mid-life is probably an impossibility in your own imagination. Part of this insecurity or lack of self-confidence is because we tend to develop a negative self-image, based on our low position on the ladder of life. People think that if they were really brilliant, they would be president of some corporation. If you were appointed president of a major corporation today, what would that do to your self-confidence?

When President Woodrow Wilson's secretary of labor died, one of the White House maids caught the president off-guard with a request: "Mr. President, my husband runs a little store on Pennsylvania Avenue and really works hard. I wonder if you would consider making him secretary of labor."

Startled by her unexpected and rather unreasonable request, the president replied, "Well, Mary, that's a very critical position. It requires a big man."

She replied, "Well, if you put my husband in that position, he'd be a big man."

Faith begins when you begin to believe in the ideas that God sends to you. Greatness does not depend upon your position in life, but upon your respect of the positive ideas that flow into your imagination! The head of a well-known company decided to test the creativity of average people and selected at random, ten uneducated persons from the bottom of the corporate ladder of one of his factories. The company president led them into the executive headquarters, had them sit in big leather chairs around a huge table, and stood before them to explain why they had been chosen: "It has come to my attention that all of you have remarkable gifts of creativity. This is the reason I called you together today. Our company is facing a problem, and I believe that you people can come up with a solution." He explained the nature of the problem and left the room for a few hours.

When he returned, he discovered that they had had a very effective brainstorming session and had, in fact, come up with a breakthrough idea! They had found an answer to the problem that had been overlooked by the top corporate research and development personnel. Obviously the executives in charge of the research and development were suffering from locked-in thinking.

The truth is that the average "bottom-of-the-ladder" person is potentially as creative as the top executive who sits in the big office. The problem is that the person on the bottom of the ladder doesn't trust his own brilliance and doesn't, therefore, believe in his own ideas.

This top executive appealed to the employees' pride and stimulated their self-respect. This is how he explains it: "Every person is creative, but a lot of people don't believe in their own creativity. When I told them they were smart, they believed it. *They came up with a solution because they were not well enough informed to know that their suggestion couldn't be done.* The rest of us never seriously considered their approach because, in our minds, it was technologically impossible. But we established their idea as a goal and were able to solve what we had assumed to be an impossible problem!"

Every human being has virtually equal creative potential.

Why isn't the average person more creative? No matter how complex the answer, one simple reason dominates. Basically, people do not believe that they are creative. Because nobody has ever told them they are creative, they have never tried to be.

Our tendency is not to do anything about the incredible ideas that come to our minds. Years later, when we read that somebody else has turned an idea into a great success, we may lament to ourselves, *I thought about that once. Why didn't I do something about it?*

As a pastor, author, and television spokesman, I find that I must constantly communicate to the masses this confidence: "All of you are brilliant!" And of course, this is true. All of us have incredible creative potential because all creative ideas come from God and all of us can tap into this wisdom.

Common people are brilliant if only they believe in their own ideas. Most human beings have the same basic brain capacity. The major difference is the attitude that a person has toward his own ideas!

At an international psychological congress in Paris, France, Dr. H. E. Gruber of Rutgers University reported that research has led to the confident belief that "child prodigies are not born, they are developed." If a child prodigy is not a genetic freak, but a product of environmental stimulation, then every human being is a potential genius. It means that somehow we have to begin to trust our better and brighter ideas. *Believe in your own brilliance!*

Faith will die in the nesting phase unless you believe in the positive ideas that drop into your mind.

A man from the Orient once traveled around the world in search of the wisest guru. He was told that this man lived in a cave high up in the Himalayas. So he loaded his horse with supplies, set off across mountains and deserts, and after months of traveling, came to the foot of a high mountain. He led his horse up the narrow path through the crevices until he came to a cave.

"Are you the guru who is known around the world for his wisdom?" he asked the old man sitting in the cave.

The old man rose to his feet, walked out into the full light of day, looked into the face of the traveler, and said, "Yes, I am known for my wisdom. What is your question?"

"Wise old man, how can I become brilliant? Where can I find wisdom?"

The wise old guru stared for a moment into the weary traveler's anxious eyes and asked in reply, "Where can you find your horse?" And with that he turned and walked back into the cave.

The answer was obvious. The traveler's horse had been with him all the time; brilliance and the capacity for wisdom had been within him all the time.

Jesus said it: "The kingdom of God is within you" (Luke 17:21). God drops ideas into your mind every day like eggs in a nest. The first stage of faith is believing in yourself.

The positive ideas that flow into your brain come from God. Don't reject the ideas simply because of your awareness of your own imperfections. Perfectionism keeps many people from ever embracing the kind of faith that could mature into a mountain-moving force.

An often-told folk tale illustrates the futility of perfectionism: A man found a beautiful pearl with one tiny flaw. He thought if he could remove that tiny imperfection, the pearl would be the world's most priceless. So he peeled off the first layer. But the flaw was still there. He took off the next layer, thinking the flaw would surely be removed, but it remained. He continued to take off layer after layer, until, finally, the flaw was gone—but so was the pearl!

Of course, no idea is perfect. No idea is without its built-in problems. But trust that the positive potential in an idea is powerful enough to merit your continued support.

The me I see is the me I'll be. To make sure you develop mountain-moving faith, build a positive self-image. If you see yourself as a person who is going to become more educated and knowledgeable, then that's precisely what you will become.

Your mind's image of yourself will release powers of self-actualization. Hold a mental picture, and it will unquestionably, invariably turn into a physical reality. Hold a negative picture, and negative results will happen. Positive results follow a positive mental picture. This is the irrevocable law of faith built by God into the universe. Draw now a positive picture of yourself, believe in your ideas, and faith will survive phase one.

2 The Testing Phase

Faith's second phase is the testing phase. No person plunges recklessly and irresponsibly ahead with every idea that moves through his brain. Ideas must be tested by asking the questions that rise out of your own value system. *Decision-making is easy if there are no contradictions in your value system.*

It's easy to make major decisions at the snap of a finger if we know the questions we have to ask to get reliable raw data as answers. A positive idea implies questions like: "Is this really necessary?" "Is it really a human need-filling idea?" "Can it be inspiring to others?"

The Crystal Cathedral, which stands on our campus, has been called a monument to possibility thinking. That could well be true. I recall very vividly the day when the bids came in while we were preparing to build the ten-million-dollar building. Suddenly we were faced with construction bids that topped fifteen million dollars! I wanted to quit.

In fact, I wrote out a news release announcing that we were aborting the project. But before I could release the story, I received two letters—one from Australia and one from Michigan.

The letter from Michigan was from a Roman Catholic nun:

Dr. Schuller, thank you for your plan to build the Crystal Cathedral. I'm on the board of directors for a hospital. We were talking about adding a wing to the hospital but the idea was voted down because the cost would run six million. I asked the members of the board, "Did you hear what Dr. Schuller is planning to build in California?" They were silent. I told them, "He is planning to raise several million dollars to build a Crystal Cathedral. If he can find several million to build a cathedral can't we find six million for a wing in a hospital?"

Dr. Schuller, that inspired all of them to reverse their decision. They went ahead and decided to build the wing and somehow solve the problem and somehow raise the money. The statement that went around the room and swayed the decision was: "If Schuller can do it, so can we."

At the same time I received a letter from an Australian minister:

Dr. Schuller, thank you for your plans to build the Crystal Cathedral. I was in a committee meeting in which the churches of Australia were contemplating building a youth ranch as a recreational and inspirational facility for young people. But the cost was going to run nearly two million dollars. Nobody believed it was possible. I asked them, "Have any of you been watching Schuller on television?" Nobody raised a hand. I told them that I'd been listening to you and that you were planning to build a Crystal Cathedral. "If he can find millions of dollars to build a cathedral, don't you think that all of us, working together, planning together, praying together, believing together, can somehow raise two million for a youth conference center?" And, Dr. Schuller, that sold the day! I'm writing to tell you the decision has not only been made, but over one million dollars has been collected! We are going to succeed. We owe it to you

How do you test the ideas that come into your mind? I test mine by this universal principle: *Will my faith, acted upon and firmly embraced, cause my life and my activity to be an inspiration to somebody else to become a better person or to achieve more in his life?* The truth is, everybody is an inspiration to somebody else. Anybody who has ever attended the Special Olympics and watched handicapped children jump over hurdles and race down the track understands what I am talking about. Suddenly tough times become good times when our positive reaction becomes an inspiration to others.

Everybody can be an inspiration to somebody else. Patty Wilson, a member of our church, was thirteen years of age when it was discovered she was epileptic. Her dad did everything he could to convince her that she shouldn't have a negative self-image because of this illness. He knew that she would encounter discrimination, that there would be those who would not hire her because she was epileptic. He knew that, without a positive self-image, she would never amount to anything. Somehow he had to communicate to her that she too could react positively to her problem and that her life would be an inspiration to others.

One day, Patty's father was driving to work when he saw a man running along the sidewalk. He wore runner's clothes, but there was something strange about his shoes. They were shaped like horses' hooves. Mr. Wilson did a double-take and threw his car into reverse. He found out that Peter Strudwick had been born with no feet. His custom-made running shoes, resembling hooves, enabled him to run. That one incident inspired Patty's dad to start running: "If he can run, so can I."

It was at this point that he vowed to teach Patty that she could be supersuccessful too. Just because she was epileptic didn't mean that she had to be handicapped. He was going to make her believe in herself. As Patty watched her dad run each morning, she became interested and was soon running alongside him. Day after day, week after week, month after month, the father-daughter team ran through the neighborhood.

Then an idea entered Patty's mind, in the nesting phase: "How can I encourage people to treat epileptics like normal people?" That question gave rise to a second idea. She found out the women's record for long-distance running and set a goal to break it. She decided to run from Orange County to San Francisco, a distance of four hundred miles, at the end of her freshman year of high school. That became her major goal, testing it on this simple principle: "Can it inspire a lot of other people, who consider themselves handicapped, to set exciting goals for themselves?" She concluded that, with enough faith, she could attain her goal and in the process inspire a lot of other people. When her faith passed from the nesting to the testing phase, she decided that she would pay the price and succeed. At that point her faith entered into the third phase.

3 The Investing Phase

The third phase of faith is the investing phase, the point at which you make a public commitment. You commit time, money, energy, and—possibly the most valuable products of all—pride and prestige to the publicly announced project. At this point many people find their faith faltering. If, by an act of will and prayer, you determine that you will make the public commitment, the odds are overwhelming that you can succeed.

Unfortunately many people let their faith die when they fail to put up the risk capital.

Patty made an investment of one year in tough training. She said, "At the end of my sophomore year I'll run from Orange County to Portland, Oregon [a distance of one thousand miles]." But she didn't stop there. "At the end of my junior year," she said, "I'll run from Orange County to St. Louis, Missouri [two thousand miles]. And at the end of my senior year, when I graduate from high school, I'll celebrate by running from Orange County, across the United States of America, to Washington, D.C. I want to shake the hand of the president of the United States."

Patty set the impossible goal of running four hundred miles from Orange County to San Francisco, California. And she made it. Of course, by that time, she had spent nearly an hour every day in training—running every morning, getting herself in top physical condition. And at the end of her second year she expanded her goal.

By this time, thousands of people were inspired by her. A book entitled *Run, Patty, Run* was published. At the end of her sophomore year, she was ready to try for Portland, Oregon.

On the day the event was to occur, Patty's high-school

*There will never be
another now—
I'll make the most
of today.*

*There will never be
another me—
I'll make the most
of myself.*

classmates stretched a big paper banner across the street. On it, they had written in red ink, "Run, Patty, run!" There were some simple ceremonies: the high-school band played, the crowd grew silent as I offered a prayer for her success, and I took a medallion from around my neck to place around hers. On the back of the medallion were the words of the Possibility Thinkers' creed: "When faced with a mountain, I will not quit. I will keep on striving until I climb over, find a pass through, tunnel underneath, or simply stay and turn the mountain into a gold mine, with God's help."

Then Patty started running, ripping through the paper banner and leaving it shredded behind her. She trotted down the road—taking the first few steps, then the first block, then the first mile. Driving behind her at a safe distance, was her mother, a registered nurse, with medication on hand, in case Patty should have a seizure. Written on the back of the van were the words, "Patty Wilson. World's Women's Long-Distance Running Record Holder. Running from California to Oregon." We followed her every day with our prayers. She did great for twenty-eight miles, when she cracked a bone in her foot. She was ready now for the fourth phase of mountain-moving faith—the arresting phase.

Before we look at the arresting phase, let me ask you; "If your problem isn't going away, have you really given it all you've got?"

If you're still unemployed, have you invested everything you possibly can in getting a job that would at least bring a dollar or two or three an hour? Remember that mountain-moving faith will never fail you, but you can fail it if you aren't willing to pay the price. You might have to pay the price of greater humility—starting back once more at the bottom of the ladder. You may have to invest more months or years in mid-life study and retraining.

When we have to back up our ideas with hard work or cold cash, it's easy to get cold feet. The going gets tough when we are forced to either put up or back out. Many people fail their faith at this third phase. They are just not faithful enough to invest everything they've got into their dream.

Try it. But get ready for the fourth phase.

4 The Arresting Phase

The nesting, the testing, the investing phases almost invariably lead to the fourth phase: the arresting phase. You've started. You've made the commitment. You've put your name on the line. You've started your run.

Now problems attack you. Troubles block you. Defeat seems certain. You begin to think you've bitten off more than you can chew. You wonder if you've made a terrible mistake with your investment. The arresting phase of faith is God's way of testing us before the final victory.

He wants to make sure: Are we really depending on Him? Will we really be grateful if we make it? Can He trust us with success? Are we going to prove humble enough to handle the big prize?

For Patty Wilson, the arresting phase came when she hurt her foot. Her parents took her to the emergency room of the hospital, praying that her injury wouldn't be serious. Doctors X-rayed her and concluded that she had, in fact, fractured her foot. One doctor told her, "Patty, you better not run. If you do, you risk permanent damage."

Patty knew there were thousands of people who were expecting her to run and complete the trip. "Doctor," she said, "if you wrapped it very tightly, don't you think I could keep running?"

"Yes, you might be able to run with the fracture if it were tightly bound," he explained. But he added, "You'll get blisters, and you can't run with blisters."

"But a blister is nothing more than water under the skin," Patty answered. "My mother's a nurse. Couldn't she just take a syringe and slip the needle into the blister and draw the water out?"

The doctor looked surprised, but said, "Yes, I suppose that might be possible." And with that, Patty had the doctor show her mother how it was to be wrapped every morning.

The arresting phase was only that. It was not terminal. It was an arresting condition. She went on and kept running—five hundred, six hundred, seven hundred, eight hundred, nine hundred, and one thousand miles. She decided to take the coastal route, not realizing that it was three hundred miles farther. She only thought that it would be far more scenic—and it was—but one thousand miles went into eleven hundred and eleven hundred to twelve hundred, and finally thirteen hundred miles brought her to the outskirts of Portland, Oregon. The governor of the state got his running suit on, joined her, and ran the last mile with her! The entire town was out to greet her. What a welcome she got! She had endured the pain. She had paid the price. She had survived the arresting period and had succeeded. She had learned that faith has incredible mountain-moving power if you will hang on and not give up when you seem to be surrounded by impossibilities.

I remember the day when I received the telephone call that an elder of my church, Stanley Reimer, had had a twenty-two minute cardiac arrest. *Twenty-two minutes?* I knew what that meant. Obviously that was a considerable amount of time during which oxygen was not reaching his brain.

They had managed to get him breathing again, but he was in what was called a "death coma." He was placed in the intensive care unit immediately, and although his body was breathing on its own, there was no other sign of life. The neurosurgeon told Stan's wife that there was no hope: "If he keeps breathing, he'll be a vegetable all of his life. He'll never close his eyes. They'll be open in a death stare exactly as you see him now."

As soon as I heard the news, I rushed to the hospital, praying all the way. "God, what will I say to him? What will I say to his wife? Will I even be able to talk to him if he is in a coma?"

I remembered that, in theological seminary, the professors had taught us: "Some day, as a pastor, you may talk to someone in a death coma. When that happens, only think *life*, only talk *life*, only believe *life*. If you are ever at the bedside of a patient who is presumed to be dying—in a 'death coma' so deep that they cannot respond in any way—keep thinking *life;* keep talking *life;* keep praying *life!* The patient may lack the power to move his lips or manifest a physical indication that he is hearing you, but his conscious and subconscious mind may in fact be getting your messages. So you must not place a negative thought in his mind.'

With that recollection I went into the intensive care unit where Stan was lying. There was Billie, his wife, standing at the bedside, tears streaming down her face. Stanley, my once-outgoing friend, looked like a statue. He could not move. From all practical appearances, he was dead. His eyes were wide open but indicated no life or responsiveness whatever. I put my arm around Billie and prayed with her. Then I took hold of Stanley's hand and I said softly, my lips close to his ear, "Stanley, I know you cannot talk. I know you cannot respond to me. But I know that, deep down within you, you can hear me. I am your pastor. This is Reverend Robert Schuller. I've just come from the church, where everyone is praying for you. And Stanley, I've got good news for you. Even though you've had a bad heart attack and are in a coma, you are going to recover. You are going to live. It's going to be a long battle. It's going to be hard and tough. But you are going to make it, Stanley!"

At that point, I had one of the most moving experiences of my life. Suddenly a tear rolled out of his staring eye! He understood! No smile; no quiver of a lip; but a tear rolled out of his eye. The doctor was shocked. Billie was shocked. One year later Stanley was able to speak full sentences. He was able to hear. His faculties were becoming normal. Today he walks and talks and laughs and is alive! A miracle, you say? Of course.

"If you have faith as a mustard seed, you will say to this mountain, 'Move . . .' and nothing will be impossible for you" (Matt. 17:20). In the darkest times, simply remind yourself that faith can move any mountain.

It was my pleasure and pride to be a close friend of the late

Senator Hubert Humphrey. When I heard that he was in New York City to have major surgery for a malignancy, I sent him a telegram. The telephone rang, and the famed senator said to me, "Hello, Bob. I'm so glad I got hold of you." His voice sounded strong. He continued, "I'm going into major surgery in just a few hours. I just wanted to thank you for your inspiring telegram. My staff just brought in a large stack of telegrams and letters, neatly pressed and sorted. I was browsing through a few of them and guess which telegram was on the top of the pile?"

I replied, "Well, obviously, the telegram from the president of the United States."

Laughing, he said, "No, Bob, yours was. I have it before me right now. I'm drawing power and strength from it this very moment. Let me read to you what you sent to me.

And he read, "God wanted me to send this Scripture verse to you: 'For I know the plans I have for you, . . . plans for good and not for evil, to give you a future and a hope" (Jer. 29:11, TLB). Later the senator would tell me that this Scripture passage gave him holding-on power in a dark time. Holding-on power is that which gives faith the strength to move mountains. For even mountains erode in time, if exposed to wind and rain.

Every project I've ever tackled has gone through its severe arresting phase. And at that point in time, you have the choice to hang on or to give up. You and you alone reserve the ultimate choice: Quit or keep believing. Which response will inspire the most people?

Tommy Lasorda, the world-famed manager of the Los Angeles Dodgers baseball team, has been a close friend of mine for many, many years. He keeps on the wall of the locker room a poem that is very familiar to many people. But it's good to reread it. After all, it's never the same poem the second or the third or the fourth time you read it. We change. Our life's situation changes and, therefore, our perception of the message changes. Here are the powerful words of Edgar A. Guest:

Don't Quit

When things go wrong, as they sometimes will,
When the road you are trudging seems all uphill,
When the funds are low and the debts are high,
And you want to smile but you have to sigh,
When care is pressing you down a bit,
Rest, if you must—but don't you quit!

Life is queer with its twists and turns,
As every one of us sometime learns,
And many a failure turns about
When he might have won had he stuck it out;
Don't give up, though the pace seems slow—
You might succeed with another blow. . . .

Success is failure turned inside out—
the silver tint of the clouds of doubt—
And you can never tell how close you are,
It may be near when it seems afar;
So stick to the fight when you are hardest hit—
It's when things get worse that you mustn't quit!

Don't trust the clouds—trust the sunshine. Don't set your compass by the flash of lightning—set it by the stars. Trust the sun—don't trust the shadows. Believe in your dreams—don't believe in your despairing thoughts. Have faith in your faith—and doubt your doubts. Trust in your hopes—never trust in your hurts. And you will move on eventually, effectively, inspiringly to faith's final phase: the cresting phase.

5 The Cresting Phase

Yes, the crowning phase of faith is the cresting phase. The mountaintop is scaled! Success finally is achieved! A habit is broken. The money starts flowing your way. The chains are loosed. The bones are healed. The doctor tells you you can go home now. You walk back into the sunshine. A broken relationship is healed. The emptiness and loneliness of life is filled with a new friend and loved one. The court case is

*Decision-making
is easy
if there are
no contradictions
in your
value system.*

settled. The economy turns around. A job opportunity comes your way. The winter passes; the spring returns. God never fails to let the sun outlive the storm. And those who keep on keeping on ultimately survive successfully and, in the process, are an incredible inspiration to others to keep bravely fighting their battles, too.

Jesus Christ's life reflects all five phases of faith. By the time He was twelve years old, He knew what God wanted Him to do in His life. He had His calling. The *nesting time* of His faith was when He realized that He had to be about His Father's business.

The *testing* phase of His faith came when He spent forty days in the wilderness being tempted by Satan.

The *investing* phase of His faith came when He spent His years walking in the plains and deserts of God's land, preaching, teaching, and investing his life's energies, thoughts, and ideas and committing His prestige to the public eye. He experienced His time of popularity. The crowds followed Him everywhere. He looked supersuccessful!

But then the *arresting* phase came for Him in the Garden of Gethsemane. Hours before He walked to His death, He prayed, "Abba, Father, all things are possible for You. Take this cup away from Me; nevertheless, not what I will but what You will" (Mark 14:36). And He was crucified. It looked like the dream was dead. Everything was coming apart. His disciples had betrayed Him, deceived Him, and deserted Him.

But then came the *cresting* phase. Easter morning came, and with it the big breakthrough. We who are Christians know that He is alive today. He rules over a kingdom of believers in this world who have been saved from their self-doubt, from their self-condemnation, from their sin and shame, into the job of serving God and our fellow human beings through creative possibility thinking.

The cresting time will come for you too if you will hold on and never believe in *never*. The storms will pass. And the birds will come out to sing again!

When
the night is past
and
the dawning of the new day
is
about to break
with
fresh hopes and dreams,
then
you will hear . . .
the singing of the birds.

When
storm clouds break
to drift away
leaving bright patches of blue
with
golden shafts of sunlight
on
flower and leaf
sparkling with fresh drops of diamond rain,
then
you will hear . . .
the singing of the birds.

Yes
there are those times and places
when
the cold winter ends.
Springtime returns.
The dark night of the soul
is dissolved in a happy daybreak.
The storm is over.
Then
you will hear . . .
the singing of the birds.

—R.H.S.

Now—Believe and You Will Achieve

Mary Crowley, president of Home Interiors, a very prosperous business, was with her husband in Nassau, the

Bahamas, some years ago. On Sunday morning, they found a local church filled with the local citizens—all black, except Mary and her husband. She tells the story of how the huge silver-haired preacher with the thundering, rusty, gravelly voice kept pounding home one theme to his people all morning: "Be somebody! God never takes time to build a nobody. Everybody God creates is created to be somebody."

The God who created you gave you a brain that's brilliant. You were able to learn to read, and you have been able to read this chapter. You have a great deal of determination. You've followed the book up to this point. The fact that you are reading these words is proof of the fact that you are cut from great cloth. You are as deserving and as capable of achieving success as any other person alive in the world today! God created you to be somebody who could be an inspiration to many people. Open your mind to receive possibility thoughts. They will come like eggs dropped in a nest. Tenderly receive them and be prepared to trust in them through the testing phase, the investing phase, the arresting phase. Never abandon the dream until you've reached the cresting phase!

9

Prayer: The Power That Pulls Everything Together Successfully

Every principle we have shared with you in these pages is a key ingredient in the recipe for success. We come now to the final and most important technique necessary for effective life management. If you've followed all the steps outlined earlier, then by now you have (1) put your problems in proper perspective, (2) applied the twelve principles of managing problems positively, (3) taken charge and control of your situation, (4) tackled impossibilities with the Ten Commandments for Possibility Thinking, (5) counted to ten and won, and (6) applied the faith that will move your mountain. But through each of these stages, undergirding and overriding all the principles we have developed in the preceding pages, there must be a steady and unfailing practice of positive prayer if you are to succeed.

God guides praying people through tough times until the beautiful breakthrough finally comes. I have recently experienced a remarkable evidence of this guidance, and I can tell the story now for the first time.

One of my toughest times came two years after the completion of the Crystal Cathedral and involved my only son. Ever since he was a young teen-ager, he felt called to commit his life to Jesus Christ and to full-time ministry.

He graduated from Hope College in Holland, Michigan, and completed his theological work in California at Fuller Seminary. He began work as a part-time assistant in our ministry and had as his great goal to "spend my life working with my dad as his associate and partner in the Crystal Cathedral."

Such was the path he chose to walk. But the relationship between my son and me was about to take an unexpected turn.

Holy Week 1981

As the meeting of the church board of the Crystal Cathedral drew to a close on Tuesday night, I turned to my son and, on impulse, said to him, "Do you have anything to report to the board?"

Caught off-guard, he heard himself say something he never had planned to verbalize. "Yes, as a matter of fact, I do." After a pause, he shocked himself and everybody else by saying, "I feel I have to resign from the church." There was a ghastly silence.

"I want to be a great preacher like my father.", I thought I saw tears in his eyes. I saw him swallow a lump in his throat. "I don't believe I'll ever be able to be the man my father is unless I walk the kind of path he walked," he continued. "I've been praying a long time, and I really believe God wants me to get out and start my own church from scratch the way Dad did."

At that point his lips trembled and his eyes brimmed with tears. In all the twenty-six years of his life, I could not remember seeing him shed tears. When he was disciplined or scolded as a child, he took the deserved punishment with a stiff upper lip.

"Please excuse me." Choking back the tears, he pushed back his chair and slipped into the adjoining restroom. All of us at the table—elders, deacons, fellow ministers—sat silently looking at each other. Finally, Bob returned. He walked out tall, ramrod straight, smiling from ear to ear, but showing a redness around his eyes.

"Excuse me for that," he continued. "All my life I envisioned being only at this church. I was only six months old when my father started it. But I feel God now wants me to leave."

At that point, twelve elders and deacons stood up and formed a living chain, arms linked, and embraced my son. We prayed that God would bless him and guide him in every decision and at every step of his way. After the time of deep prayer, I looked at him and asked, "What are you thinking of doing?"

"I think there is room for another wonderful positive Protestant church in the southern part of this county," he said, "and I'm praying that God will lead me there if that is what He wants."

The meeting swiftly adjourned; it was nearly ten o'clock at night. Before my son left the room, I asked, "Bob, can we get together tomorrow?"

"Yes," he answered, "I'd like that. I have to go down to San Diego. Maybe you could ride with me."

I left a note on my secretary's desk, instructing her to cancel all of my appointments for the next day, explaining that an emergency was taking me out of town. Being with Bob was the most important thing I had to do.

The next morning we left the church together, to begin the ninety-mile trip south. We'd been traveling for about eighteen miles when I said, "Bob, starting a new church from scratch, as you hope to do, is a lot tougher today than when I was a young minister a quarter of a century ago."

Bob looked at me and stopped me properly with this statement: "Then maybe you'd better stop preaching your possibility thinking, Dad!"

He had me, and I had no retort. "But where do you expect to buy land today, Bob?" I asked, adding, "You know when I started this church, we were able to buy land for six thousand dollars an acre. Today there isn't much vacant land to be bought. And if you can find an empty parcel, it would cost you over one hundred thousand dollars an acre!"

He raised his right arm and with one long finger pointed through the window to the huge expanse of undeveloped ranch land directly in line with our car. An American flag flew from a flagpole on a sloping green hillside surrounded by palm trees. It was the famous ninety-two-acre Rancho Capistrano.

"I have thought and prayed, and I believe that God is going to give me a piece of that land," Bob said confidently. I was floored by his powerful, affirmative faith.

"Why, Bob, that might just be possible," I answered, for the first time getting a little excited about his dream. "After all, that's where John Crean lives, and he's the man who gave the first million dollars to launch the Crystal Cathedral fund drive. In fact, it was in that house, in that grove under the American flag, that I had asked John for a lead-off gift that would be big enough to guarantee the successful launching of the Crystal Cathedral campaign.

"You know, Bob," I continued, getting more and more enthusiastic, "I remember now that John said to me once, 'I don't know what I'm going to do with this big ninety-two-acre ranch. But I guess God has a plan for it. I know I don't intend to keep living here all my life.' You know, Bob, he just might give you a few acres."

"I'm sure he will," Bob said. "I've prayed about it, and I feel strongly, without an ounce of doubt, that that is exactly what God has in mind."

"Then make a date with John and approach him," I said. "It's your job, you know, not mine."

By the end of the day on Wednesday, we had made our trip to San Diego and returned home. Shortly after the sunset of this day in Holy Week, my son called John Crean for an appointment "to get together and talk."

"How about tomorrow?" Mr. Crean offered.

"Sounds great," said Bob.

The next day—Maundy Thursday—they met for lunch. Bob called me at breakfast and said, "I'm having lunch with John Crean. Pray for me."

"Bob," I said, "do you realize that it was on Maundy Thursday five years ago that I sat down with him and asked him to give the first million-dollar gift? Now on Maundy Thursday

*Brownouts
do not
have to be
burnouts.*

five years later, you'll ask him to make possible the birth of a new church. But don't be surprised if he says no, Bob, and don't be discouraged. After all, he said no the first time I asked him to give a million dollars. It was only after he prayed it through that he came back and made the gift."

I couldn't wait for Thursday afternoon to get the word from my son. The phone rang late in the afternoon.

Bob's voice had a quality about it that I had never heard before: "Dad, you'll never guess what John Crean has done."

"Tell me quickly," I demanded.

"Well, I asked him if I could have a small chunk of the ranch to start a church. He said to me, 'Bob, you're too late. Last night Donna and I gave away the entire ranch to somebody else.'"

It was the biggest shock of my son's life and a bigger shock to me.

John Crean went on to explain to my son that for more than ten years he had found health, healing, and spiritual strength by attending retreats sponsored by the Jesuits. Few, if any, organizations in the world are more experienced in running retreats effectively than the Jesuits.

"Donna and I prayed and came to the conclusion that God wanted the ranch to be a retreat center. Since the Jesuits really know how to run retreats, we have offered it to them. In fact, we signed the papers last night, deeding the entire ninety-two-acre ranch to them."

It was good news and bad news. The good news was that John Crean was giving the land to a wonderful organization of godly men for a fantastic cause. The bad news was my fear of what it might do to my son's faith in God's guidance through answered prayer. Meanwhile, I had a dream I had never shared with anyone. I had long dreamed of having a retreat center. Now, I was also spiritually distraught at having lost the opportunity to acquire a piece of property on which I would have been able to have fulfilled my unspoken dream of launching retreats for married couples, burned-out ministers, or persons with problems with alcoholism.

Mr. Crean was a voting and an active member of the "Hour

of Power" program's board of directors, but I had never shared my secret dream with him. He never had known of my heart's desire. Naturally, there was no reason why he should consider offering the property to us. Had he known how deeply I had wanted to get into this healing ministry myself, maybe he would have offered part of it to the Crystal Cathedral and part to the Jesuits. We could have made a little chunk available for a church site for my son. Was it too late? Perhaps we could purchase a part of it from the Jesuits. I picked up the telephone on Saturday and called Mr. Crean. "Is your gift of the ranch carved in granite, or poured in concrete? And, if so, is the cement dry?"

"Oh, yes, I'm afraid it is, Bob," he answered. "You know, the ranch is worth nearly ten million dollars and I'm giving it to them without any strings attached, so I'm sure they will accept it. They are very enthusiastic about it, or I wouldn't have signed the gift conveyance.

"Of course, they have to sign the papers to legally accept the gift. All I've asked is that they get the signed papers notarized and sent to me within the next six months. After all, I do want to have it all taken care of before we get into the last quarter of the year when I will have to calculate my own tax situation."

I was quiet for a moment before I said, "I wish I had known that you wanted to turn it into a retreat center, John. I had secret dreams myself. But I am sure you did the right thing, for you are a man of prayer. I know that. I've never met a man that prays more sincerely than you do, John."

With that I hung up, but my heart was enormously heavy. We would not be able to use Rancho Capistrano for the renewal conference grounds of which I had secretly dreamed. I had hoped to get to that project after the Crystal Cathedral was finished. It had taken nearly ten years to conceive, promote, develop, and construct the Crystal Cathedral! Now in my mid-fifties, that project was completed and I wanted to get into the development of the conference facilities. But the only potential piece of property that might have been available to me had been given to someone else.

July 1981

Three months passed after the Creans had signed the papers giving the property to the Jesuits. John Crean invited friends, relatives, and leaders of the Jesuit community to his ranch for a special birthday party where he announced to everyone that the gift was being given and was being accepted. The Jesuits moved in a brass cross, candles, and a communion set, using the pool table in the game room as a place for their private morning Mass.

August 1981

"I am going to need the gift accepted, signed, and notarized," John Crean told a prominent Jesuit official. But for some reason the signed papers didn't come back. There were, after all, internal considerations that needed clarification by several important persons at different levels in the hierarchy.

Crean unburdened his heart to me: "I have never worked so hard to try to give a gift away. I don't know why they haven't signed the papers and accepted it. I wish I had given it to you, Bob, but it's too late."

September 1981

"The six months will be up on Monday," Mr. Crean instructed his attorney. "Please write to the Jesuits and tell them that I will need to have the papers accepting my gift signed and notarized by 4:00 P.M. on Monday, September 4. If I do not receive an acceptance at the end of this six-month period of time, I will feel directed by God to dispose of it another way."

On Monday, September 4, I was in my library when the telephone rang at 4:04 P.M. It was Donna Crean, John's wife:

"Bob, I wondered if you could drop around tonight. John would like to talk to you."

"Donna, you know this is Monday. Monday night is my date night. You know my wife and I never go anywhere on Monday nights except on our date."

"I know that, Bob," she answered. "Maybe you could just drop around the ranch on the way out to dinner. It won't take long. Let me give you a hint of what John wants to talk about. The gift of the ranch fell through, and he'd like to give it to you "

I cried; I squealed; I almost fainted!

Two hours later, Arvella and I were sitting in the same room of the same house where five years before I had asked a total stranger to give a one-million-dollar gift to launch an incredible project to be called the Crystal Cathedral. Now I was in the same room to receive the gift of a ninety-two-acre ranch.

"John," I said, with quivering voice, "you know this is an answer to prayer. It all started when my son, in prayer, asked for a place to start his church."

At that point, John Crean interrupted, strongly and intensely. "Bob, I am giving this to you for a retreat center and for your church purposes. It is not for young Bob. He has to earn his own way. He has to experience his own struggles. It is my dream that this will be a retreat center, not just another church."

I had to respect his strong feelings, but, at the same time, I was crushed inside. What would I tell my son? I would not have been sitting in that room receiving that gift on that night, if my son had not first pointed the way out of his own prayer experiences

November 1981

My son accepted the fact that his father was the beneficiary of the ranch and that he would never be able to have even one acre of it for a church. He searched unsuccessfully for an empty hall. He tried to use a drive-in theater, but the city council rejected his application, contending that it would create too big a traffic problem. He looked for a warehouse to rent. None was available. He finally found a college gymnasium, and in November 1981, he started a church service, hoping some people would come. The crowd grew slowly but strongly, through December, January, February. Meanwhile, the ranch stood idle. I had lost my enthusiasm for its development.

March 1982

John Crean and I met and agreed that we needed to have a long talk about developing the ranch. "Let's spend two or three days together on the boat," he offered. I agreed. "You know, I am very impressed with the job young Bob has done," he said, as we sailed the Pacific, looking for marlin. "My brother has been going to young Bob's church. He has joined it, did you know that?" Crean asked. He turned and looked at me, continuing, "A lot has happened during the last year. Young Bob has proven himself. If he'd like to use the old barn at the other end of the property, make it into a little chapel, and have his church meet there, I think that might work out O.K."

He went on: "Donna and I have been praying, and we believe in the principles practiced by the members of Alcoholics Anonymous: 'Let go and let God.' Totally relinquish and release your entire position to God Almighty. Let Him do exactly what He wants to do the way He wants to do it, in your life. We feel we have to do that as far as the ranch is concerned. Do what you want, in the way you want, Bob. I believe you will pray for guidance; I believe God will guide you; and I believe you will do the right thing as you follow Him."

No sooner had John Crean made that profound spiritual profession than a surge of release and inner strength came to me. I can only describe it as the reality of God flowing through my mind and my mood.

Today, as this book is published, my son is holding church services in what was the barn on the ninety-two-acre ranch. Two services with growing audiences are worshiping God in this newborn church! The first of three carefully designed retreat centers is under construction. The beautiful rolling ranch land with a private lake, lovely woods, trees, and waterfalls will be preserved as a Garden of Eden—a place where tired and burned-out souls and marriages can find renewal and new life!

Two years have passed since my son first prayed and was pointed to the ranch. Two years after his prayer, he is holding services on the property that he was led by faith through prayer to claim in the name of God.

His faith went through every phase—the nesting phase when God dropped the idea; the testing phase when he asked whether this was indeed the best and only place; the investing phase; the arresting phase when he was told he could not use it, and, today, he is enjoying the cresting phase of faith.

The times of hope, despair, enthusiasm, and depression have all passed. Today the sun is shining. The sky is blue. The dream has come true!

And I have just finished writing a letter to the Jesuits:

My dear brothers in Christ,

You have been relieved of the responsibility of maintaining and managing the ranch. We have accepted that awesome responsibility. And in a few months we'll have luxurious bedroom facilities, chapel facilities, and dining facilities available for you, my good brothers, to come for a retreat if you find the rooms suitable.

After all, we do not own the land. God owns it. We have only been made stewards and caretakers of it. And all human beings are God's children. All of us are brothers. If we can be of service to you, please let me know.

As this book goes to press, I am just beginning what I expect to be a five-year project of developing the gardens and the structural facilities of the Rancho Capistrano Renewal Center. It will be a project that I expect will keep me creatively occupied with peak enthusiasm. After that, I expect to spend the rest of my life using the place to erase tensions, fears, sins, and stress from the hearts of those who come to the place where the swallows come back every spring.

There will be one Bible verse etched in stained glass dominating this entire garden renewal center. It is the promise of God found in the Song of Solomon: "And the time of the singing of the birds has come" (2:12; paraphrased).

The storm has passed. The birds are singing. The night is over. Tough times never last. Tough people do! That's really true if we live moment by moment, day by day, in complete surrender to God in prayer. Through prayer, God gives the power to hold on to tough times until the breakthrough comes.

But those who wait on the LORD
Shall renew their strength;
They shall mount up with wings like eagles,
They shall run and not be weary,
They shall walk and not faint
(Is. 40:31).

I have found immense strength through this promise of God. As I wait upon Him in prayer I find the strength to go on. The terrible danger in tough times is that we lose our emotional power to remain enthusiastic and creative. But the solution God offers is prayer, the power that pulls everything together successfully.

Prayer—The Power That Pulls Everything Together Successfully

We all know what it means to be burned out. There are people who get burned out professionally, creatively. There are institutions that get burned out productively. There are families and marriages that get burned out. There are individual personalities that lose their enthusiasm for life.

The problem with burnouts is that they inevitably lead to crash landings.

I don't want to see your life crash about you. Neither does God. That's why He's given us a solution to the burnout problem. His solution is prayer.

When times are the toughest and it seems as if you are as low as you can go and when possibility thinking hasn't had the results you expected, you are in danger of burnout. It's precisely at these times you need God because when you remain in touch with God, you are immune to burnout. You say, "But don't you get terribly down at times?" Yes, but remember I said you can be immune to *burnouts* not *brownouts*. A brownout is a temporary power failure. It is not a permanent resignation, divorce, or bill of sale. You may feel down in a brownout, but you don't abandon the ship as you would in a burnout. It's important to know the difference. In a brownout the power will come back on. A burnout? That's a toughie. To keep a brownout from becoming a burnout you must remain in touch with God—and that's what prayer is. But remember, keeping in touch with God won't eliminate your problems . . . it will only help you manage them. The late comedian Grady Nutt said it: "God should be a resource in the struggle, not a way around it."

How do you renew your strength and spirit during a brownout time? How do you pick yourself up in time to prevent a burnout and prove the truth of this book: *tough times never last, but tough people do!*? Let's look at the word *renew.* I'm going to deal with each of the five letters that make up the word *renew* in the hopes that you will know and will remember how to renew yourself whenever you feel you're about to burn out.

R Review your past.

Where have I come from? What was keeping me going? Review the persons that have been in your life, close to you, as well as the projects and problems you faced. Review your private practices, your philosophy of life, your value system, and your religion.

Review what was the source of your emotional energy. What turned you on in the past? Why aren't you excited now? Was it a special person or a project that inspired you before? Has the person left or is the project now complete?

Or were you being challenged by a problem, and the problem is now solved? Perhaps you were challenged by an adversary. The spirit of competition motivated you.

Was it a private or public life-style that kept you going? Have you forsaken your ideals? Have you accommodated yourself to questionable ethics or a dubious moral standard? And is this like a silent termite eating away the youthful enthusiasm?

Was it a false expectation that enticed you and led you onward and upward? Shakespeare said that many of our goals in life are really like needles in haystacks: "You shall seek all day until you find them, and when you find them they are not worth the search."

Too often our goals rise from a defective value system. And the energy to remain enthusiastic in life, marriage, and career is often drawn from the search and the hunt rather than from the final harvest and the ultimate ingathering.

What was the taproot of your positive emotion that kept your light burning through the years? Review your life carefully.

Examine all the possibilities.

What would you set as your goals if . . . ? What would you do if you had the money, if you had the education, if you had the training, if you had the contacts, if you had the support base? What would you do if you had the marketing system, if you had the right people on your team? What would you do if you had the time, if you had the plant, if you had the equipment? What would you do if you knew it could not fail?

There are far more possibilities than you think. Examine them.

N Name the price you're willing to pay.

Are you willing to go to school for two or three years? Are you willing to move? Are you willing to go through six to eight months of physical therapy to walk again? Name the price you're willing to pay.

When Henry Ford transported Thomas Edison's entire laboratory to Dearborn Village, he also brought the trash pile. Why? Because he wanted everybody to see how much Edison had to throw away in order to finally have some success. Every sales person knows this. There's always a pile of rejections in order to get the "yes." What price are you willing to pay?

When I first saw the model of the Crystal Cathedral, I said to my wife, "That is fantastic! If giving leadership to the development of that cathedral would cost the price of high blood pressure and even a fatal heart attack, I'd gladly pay it for that building." I meant it. When you feel that deeply about something you are going to make it.

E Elect the best possibility, no matter what the price.

Choose the best; shun mediocrity. Mediocrity has a way of shriveling up enthusiasm. But commitment to excellence taps an incredible source of energy. Elect the best, no matter what the price tag.

W Wait and work.

Probably nothing is more difficult than to keep waiting, working, plodding, and maintaining patience through dark times. But we must. And in God's good time, hope and help will come our way. Oftentimes someone's unexpected, off-the-cuff comment or curt answer to an important question can be the breakthrough to a new emotional sunrise.

Henry Ford was born on a farm, left the farm at the age of sixteen, and got a job as a mechanic in Detroit. Then he became a fireman in the Detroit Edison Company and worked his way up until he became the chief engineer. Of course, Edison was just a big name to him. When Thomas Edison was visiting the company, Henry Ford told himself that if he ever got close enough to this famous inventor, he would ask him one question. Ford got the chance in 1898. He stopped Edison and said, "Mr. Edison, may I ask you a question? Do you think gasoline is a good fuel source for motor cars?" Edison had no time for Ford; he simply said yes and walked away. And that was it. But that answer turned Ford on. Henry Ford made a commitment. It was in 1909, eleven years later, that he turned out the Tin Lizzy. He took criticism, but during those eleven years he worked and he waited, and he waited and he worked. He experienced brownouts, but never burnouts.

"Those who wait on the Lord shall renew their strength." The Lord might strengthen you through some person, or a chance meeting. It may come through someone God uses to encourage you. I know this is true because there have been times when I needed to be encouraged. And there have been other times when God used me to give encouragement to someone else. "Wait on the Lord." Remain in touch with God through prayer.

You've heard of Florence Nightingale. But did you know that she was born to wealth and social prominence in London, England? This brilliant young girl from a socially prominent, wealthy family wrote in her diary in 1851 at the age of thirty-one, "I see nothing that I desire today, other than death." She came close to burning out. But she renewed herself. How? She *reviewed* her life. Money, social position didn't do anything for her. Then she *examined* the possibilities. If only she could help people. She wanted to be a nurse. Her mother and father said that such a status was beneath their dignity. But she *named* the price. She was willing to be ostracized by her parents and society. She *elected* to be a nurse. Her mother wrote, "We are two ducks, my husband

and I, and we've given birth to a wild swan." But Florence Nightingale's biographer said, "The mother was so wrong, for Florence was not a wild swan but an eagle." The Crimean War broke out. Florence chose to go. "Possessed by demons," her family said. "Victim of a nervous breakdown." She was ostracized, criticized, considered insane. But for three years she waited and worked among the dying men, their blood, their amputated legs. She came home three years later in 1859, and she wrote and published notes on how hospitals should be operated. And she changed hospitals. You and I have the benefits of it a century or more later.

"Wait on the Lord" in prayer and He will renew a dream. And a brownout will give way to a light-up.

Brownouts are not necessarily burnouts. Tough times pass. Tough people survive. If there is only one principle you remember after you put this book down, let it be this: Brownouts do not have to be burnouts.

It's terribly important that we hang on in the face of hope and never call a brownout a burnout. If we do quit, we will later on look back and say, "I realize now it was just a phase—just a period of time—just a natural transition I was going through. I shouldn't have packed up; I should have seen myself through it. When the kids were all little with all the diapers, that was an age. When the company was young and struggling and I had to do my own secretarial and janitorial work, that was an era. Those times would not have lasted forever.

Every institution, every individual, every job has its ages, passages, periods, eras; we have to be careful to hold on. When the brownout is only a brownout and not a burnout, the power will come back on. When there is a temporary overload on the emotional system, we must rest, wait upon the Lord, and the new dawning will come.

The most dangerous thing in the world is to make an irreversible negative decision during a brownout time. Don't sell your real estate because there is no electricity in the building. It's just a brownout, not a burnout. Never cut a dead tree down in the wintertime. I remember one winter my dad needed firewood, and he found a dead tree and sawed it down. In the spring to his dismay new shoots sprouted around the trunk. He said, "I thought sure it was dead. The leaves had all dropped in the wintertime. It was so cold that twigs snapped as surely as if there were no life left in the old tree. But now I see that there was still life at the taproot." He looked at me and said, "Bob, don't forget this important lesson. Never cut a tree down in the wintertime." Never make a negative decision in the low time. Never make your most important decisions when you are in your worst mood.

Wait. Be patient. The storm will pass. The spring will come. New feelings will come over you, and they will be positive. Keep waiting affirmatively and positively in prayer for God's strength to return.

In the early days of our church history, I went through a prolonged period of two years when an associate minister was conspiring to replace me as the senior minister of the young church. He managed to attract several of his supporters from the church board. They had secret meetings during the week. I knew this was going on and didn't know how to handle it. I abhor confrontations. My natural inclination was to pack up and split.

Yet, I was the senior minister assigned by the denomination with the responsibility of getting the church organized. I was reared to be responsible and accountable. "You never go fishing until you've done the chores," my father used to say to me.

I couldn't possibly leave the church with the job undone. I had to hold on. It was not a burnout time, but it was surely a brownout time. I slipped cards with inspirational thoughts written on them under the glass top of my desk. One was a statement Jesus made: "No one, having his hand to the plow, and looking back, is fit for the kingdom of God" (Luke 9:62).

Another sentence was written by a Dr. Butler of Baylor University: "When things get rough don't move. People and pressures shift, but the soil remains the same no matter where you go."

Wait on the Lord, and He will strengthen your heart!

I have had my brownout times. I still get them from time to time. Today I find my life is highly visible. I have made the discovery from personal experience that when someone's work achieves high visibility through the publication of books or through television appearances, he will be vulnerable to a wide interpretation by people and institutions who may or may not understand and interpret him correctly. It has never been easy, and it remains difficult for me today to keep going with enthusiasm when erroneous and negative interpretations are made of my work.

I have learned that if you are a leader, you will be called upon to be the front person. "The point man" is what they call it in the military service. And the point man is always at the top of the needle. It is impossible to be at the top of the needle without getting pricked.

I find that encouragement and sincere compliments are a major source of encouragement to me. They keep my light bright. When they are replaced by cynical criticisms from people who are probably ill-informed, ill-motivated, or uneducated, I must return to my Ultimate Source. In prayer I must return to God who gives me my direction and orders and keep going, for prayer is the power that pulls everything together successfully.

In the *Reader's Digest*, December 1982, a marvelous little piece of philosophy appeared that may be helpful at this point. It is entitled "Anyway."

People are unreasonable, illogical and self-centered.
Love them anyway.

If you do good, people will accuse you of selfish
  ulterior motives.
Do good anyway.

If you are successful, you will win false friends
  and true enemies.
Succeed anyway.

Honesty and frankness make you vulnerable.
Be honest and frank anyway.

The good you do today will be forgotten tomorrow.
Do good anyway.

The biggest people with the biggest ideas can be shot down by
the smallest people with the smallest minds.
Think big anyway.

People favor underdogs but follow only top dogs.
Fight for some underdogs anyway.

What you spent years building may be destroyed overnight.
Build anyway.

Give the world the best you have and you'll get kicked in the
teeth.
Give the world the best you've got anyway.[1]

The point of this piece of philosophy is that you should
find joy and light in doing God's will regardless of how people will interpret it or accept it. Above all, "to thine ownself
be true." Wait on the Lord, and *He will renew Your strength!*

Prayer is the umbilical cord that allows you—with your
embryonic ideas—to draw nourishment from a source that
you, like an unborn infant, can neither see nor fully know or
comprehend—God our heavenly Father! Prayer is the power
that pulls everything together successfully.

With this prayerful attitude, tackle your problem today.
Turn it over to God. Take out a sheet of paper. Pick up a
pencil. And get ready for the ideas that He will drop into
your mind. Together let's get ready for action!

[1]Reprinted with permission from the December 1982 *Reader's Digest* and RESPONSE, a
newsletter of Presbyterian Church of White Plains, White Plains, NY, Marjorie
W. Timmons, editor.

PART
III

*Beginning
Is Half Done!*

10

Alphabet For Action

In difficult times, people too often lose the ability to face the future optimistically. They begin to think about their tomorrows negatively.

They forget that the tough times will pass. They concentrate on the problems of today rather than on the opportunities of tomorrow. In so doing, they not only lose the potential of today, they also throw away the beauty of tomorrow. That's the real tragedy of tough times.

Frank Sinatra said it: "Dr. Schuller, your messages are medicine to my mind. Somehow, every time I listen, I have the courage to step into tomorrow."

I have to give credit where credit is due. I wish *I* had thought of those words: ". . . the courage to step into tomorrow." If there were one thing I could give to every person, it would be the courage to step into tomorrow. Probably you are not in need of opportunities; they are already there. You just have to have the courage to step into tomorrow and grasp them.

It doesn't matter how young or how old you are—if you want your life to thrive you must have the courage to step into tomorrow.

Last week, a six-year-old boy came to me and said, "Dr. Schuller, may I have your autograph? And will you write something special? I'm going to be a preacher too when I grow up." Isn't that sensational? Six years old, and he has a plan.

I'll never forget Grandma Finley. I met her one summer while I was working on the Campus Afloat Ship, connected with Chapman College in Orange, California. I was acting as professor of philosophy and history. In our student body was Mrs. Finley.

We all called her "Grandma Finley" because she was eighty-four years old. She had been traveling worldwide since the end of the Second World War. As I recall, her trips had included six visits to the Soviet Union.

Word of her reached the people in New Zealand, and so when our ship docked in Auckland, the press was waiting to meet Grandma Finley.

I happened to overhear the interview. A reporter said, "Grandma Finley, is it true you've had six trips through Russia?"

"Yes."

"Is it true that you've been traveling to a different country every year, for thirty-four years?"

She said, "Yes."

"And is it true you're eighty-four years old?"

"Yes."

And then the reporter said, "Well, I suppose this is your last cruise."

She was offended, shocked, and upset. She said, "The last cruise? Of course not! I belong to the CMT Club."

"What's the CMT Club?"

"That's the 'Can't Miss a Thing Club.' I'm not going to miss a thing. My bus is leaving. Good-bye." She took off, trotting halfway to the bus.

Whether you are six or eighty-four years old, you have a tomorrow. You can choose to face it positively—and make the most of it—or you can throw it away.

Recently, while I was in New York, I rode in a cab from downtown Manhattan to Long Island. During the hour-long ride, I worked on the message I was to give. I took out my daily itinerary for my three-day visit to the city and began to make notes on the back.

I looked over the notes I'd just made. In frustration and dissatisfaction I tore off the page with what I'd written, put it on the seat, and started over. I wrote down my thoughts on the next page of my itinerary. I was pleased with my new efforts.

When I reached my destination and got out of the car, I suddenly remembered that the piece of paper I'd left on the seat of the cab was my itinerary for the next day. I said, "Hey, I've got to keep that." As I retrieved it, I added, "I almost threw away part of tomorrow!"

Maybe that's your problem. Maybe you've thrown away part of your tomorrow. Perhaps you've had a dynamic idea on which you've neglected to capitalize. You've carelessly tossed it aside.

Every idea is worth considering. Most ideas are worthy of action. The most tragic waste is the waste of a good idea. I ask you now: Is there some great idea in your life that you have still not dealt with affirmatively?

Everyone has within him some idea of something that he should have started but hasn't. Maybe it's to quit smoking. Maybe it's to lose weight. Maybe it's to get started on a physical fitness program. Maybe it's to join a church. Maybe it's to accept Jesus Christ as your Savior and Lord. Maybe it's to read the Bible, which you may never have done. Maybe it's to start a new business. Maybe it's to go back to school. Maybe it's to take a positive attitude toward your marriage, discarding the negative attitude you've had far too long. Maybe it's to quit drinking. I don't know what it is, but everyone, I have no doubt, has an idea of some area in which he should be taking some action for self-improvement. It's a great idea.

Now—what will you do with that idea? America is known for its waste. We waste money, energy, gasoline, fuel, time, clothing, and paper. But nothing is as tragic as the waste of a good idea! So, if there's a good idea in your mind right now, don't waste it!

How do you keep from wasting it? Very simply, begin to do something about it!

When I took a course in English composition, I confess that I received a very low grade. My teacher said, "Bob Schuller, I think you can make a living by talking; you're a good talker. But don't ever try to write." God bless her.

I remembered her negative thought when something stirred inside me some years ago, suggesting I put my thoughts into writing. I felt sure I should write a book. But I thought, *I can't write a book. Smarter people than I have told me I'd never be able to.* And then I remembered: Beginning is half done. So I took out a piece of paper and typed, *"Move Ahead With Possibility Thinking* by Robert Schuller." I bought a loose-leaf binder and stuck the title sheet in it. Beginning is half done! Before I knew it, I had written a book!

Just because you're flunking something doesn't mean you *can't* pull good marks in it.

Since then, the level of my accomplishment is due, in large measure, to that one sentence. Beginning is half done! Get started! Winning starts with beginning!

What kind of a person are you? Often we hear the question: How do you treat people? A far more important question is this: How do you treat ideas?

Treat ideas like newborn babies.

Treat them tenderly . . .
    They can get killed pretty quickly.
Treat them gently . . .
    They can be bruised in infancy.
Treat them respectfully . . .
    They could be the most valuable things
    that ever came into your life.
Treat them protectively . . .
    Don't let them get away.
Treat them nutritionally . . .
    Feed them, and feed them well.
Treat them antiseptically . . .
    Don't let them get infected with the germs
    of negative thoughts.

Treat them responsibly!
    Respond! Act! Do something with them!
              —R.H.S.

How do you treat good ideas? By *acting* on them, that's
how!

Decide to Decide

You handle ideas by making some kind of a decision. Winning starts with beginning! And to begin, you must do something *now*.

What do you do when you have a good idea? Just observe
how differently people respond to ideas:

1. Insecure people hibernate. They run away from good
ideas. They're afraid they might fail or that they might have to
spend too much effort. And, like a bear which feels the first
whisper of a winter wind and rushes off, tail between his legs,
to hide out until the sun comes back months later, some people
hibernate.

2. Lazy people luxuriate. They don't pay much attention
to ideas. They want to enjoy the pleasures of this life. They'll
get serious later on, probably when they're old. Maybe
they'll even get religion.

3. Wounded people commiserate. They say, "Oh, it's a
good idea, but I couldn't do it. I've tried it so often. I've tried
to lose weight. I've tried all kinds of diets, but I keep getting
fatter." Or, "I've tried to quit smoking twenty times in my
life, and I've even torn up the package of cigarettes and
thrown it in the wastebasket." Or, "I've tried to quit drinking,
but I can't." Or, "I've tried to get along with my wife, but we
still argue." Don't commiserate.

4. Foolish people procrastinate. They put off acting on
their ideas. "Later on, when I'm ready, I'll do something
about it," they say. "I'm not ready yet." Let me give you a
sentence that could change your life: Don't wait until you're
ready to make big decisions, or you'll never accomplish half

of what you could. The difference between the high achiever and the low achiever is this: The high achiever almost always makes decisions before he's ready to move.

Who would honestly say he was ready for marriage when he got married? When I look back, I realize I was not. And the day I joined the church, as a young boy of sixteen, in a balcony in a northwest Iowa country church, I heard the minister say, "Today is the day of salvation." And I thought, *That's right, Reverend. You really are right.* I don't know what came over me, but I got out of that pew and gave my life to Jesus Christ. But you know, I wasn't ready for the challenges, the temptations, the problems that I was to run into. Don't wait until you're ready, or you'll never make the move!

5. Wise people dedicate. They're do-it-now people. No grass grows under their feet. That's why they don't waste the most precious thing in the world—a good idea. They don't waste a good moment or a good opportunity.

How do you handle your good ideas? Don't hibernate. Don't luxuriate. Don't commiserate. Don't procrastinate. Dedicate yourself to that idea that has come from God. And then you can become the person you want to be!

How do you dedicate? How do you get started? Let me give you this clue: Don't wait for an inspiration. Use your head, and your heart will follow. Don't wait until you feel like it to make the move. If you wait until you feel like it, emotion will run you instead of reason. Many times two people who rationally know they belong together marry and develop love, where love did not exist.

Frequently I tackled an idea and said, "I'm going to do something about it," although I didn't feel like it. When I started writing this book, I did not feel like it! If I had waited until I got inspired, nothing would have happened. A published author will tell you how to write. Simply set a specific time to go to the typewriter and type. And you may not feel like it when you start, but pretty soon the inspiration comes.

You may need to go on a diet, but you don't feel like dieting. You're waiting until you feel like it. Don't! Discipline

*Beginning
is
half done!*

yourself for one full day, and then for two days, and do you know what? After two days you'll feel like it! Use your head, and your heart will follow!

I've learned another thing: I can do anything I think I can . . . but I can't do anything alone. I've taught this, preached it, written it, and tried it, and it's true. I always need someone to support me! Don't try to handle your dreams alone. It won't work.

Winning starts with beginning, and beginning starts with a single action.

Do something great with a great idea. Whatever it is that you should be doing—a concept for self-improvement, a dream, a goal, or a commitment to Jesus Christ—I want you to do it. Decide that this is going to be the day you're going to do something about it!

Life today is nothing more than a collection of results of the choices you have made. And I would now add this sentence: Today's decisions are tomorrow's realities.

Plan your future because you have to live in it. That means that you must be mature enough to change your mind. Show me a person who never changes his mind, and I'll show you a very immature, childish, stubborn person.

To really succeed in life, all you have to do is (1) get started! and (2) never quit. Those are the only two hurdles you need to clear to become the person God wants you to be!

Let me call your attention to a powerful Bible verse: "For [God] says: 'In an acceptable time I have heard you,/ And in the day of salvation I have helped you.'/Behold, now is the accepted time; behold, now is the day of salvation" (2 Cor. 6:2).

You didn't think when you got up this morning that this would be the day your life would change, did you? But it's going to happen because the only thing that stands between you and grand success in living are these two things: Getting started and never quitting! You can solve your biggest problem by getting started, right here and now.

Together you and I are going to create an *alphabet for action.*

For each letter of the alphabet we will assign a possibility-thinking verb—not a noun, not an adjective, but a verb. Verbs are action words, and this is an alphabet for action. For example, here are some verbs that start with *A*.

Attack your problem with courage and your possibility with enthusiasm.

Ask the *market* what needs are undeveloped; the *masters* how to develop a new product; your *mind and heart* what your real motives are and what price you're willing to pay.

Add up your strength. You can see. You can hear. You can read. You can telephone. You are stronger than you think you are.

Adjust your mind to the changing times. You'll never begin until you get with it.

Accept the irrevocable negative realities. And accept the fact that you can be successful—somewhere, somehow, someway—anyway. I have a friend, David Wong in Hong Kong, who keeps this slogan on his desk: "Hallelujah anyway!"

As you move through this alphabet, I want you to think of your own verbs. I will give you one in each case and leave blanks where you can add your own. Earnestly pray that God will give you the right verb (it may or may not be the same verb I suggest). Then take the action that will lead you down the path that He wants you to walk. With God's Holy Spirit leading your life and your mind, you will help write this closing chapter. You and God will join in the final authorship. Then truly this book will be an answer to the prayer: "Lord, give me the guidance to know when to hold on and when to let go and the grace to make the right decision with dignity. Amen."

Whatever words you choose, remember this: *Pick positive, not negative, words.* Positive words provoke positive results. Negative words promote negative results. The difference? How can you tell positive words? You can feel them.

Yes, you can feel the mood they generate. Positive words inspire positive emotions: *humor, courage, optimism, faith, con-*

fidence. Whereas negative words stimulate negative emotions: *suspicion, fear, distress, anger, doubt, depression, sadness, worry, jealousy.*

Remember this: *The words you choose will change your mood for better or worse.* Architects say, "The client shapes the structure—from then on the structure shapes the client [the occupant]." Carefully censor the words, and you'll be molding and manipulating creatively and constructively your mental attitude and your personality. You and only you will design and shape your personality. Make it great and joyous. For you'll have to live in it. From then on, your personality will shape your destiny. The right words will manage or mangle you. Choose them carefully and positively.

A Affirm

Affirm that you can do it. You can find a job. You can change careers. You can learn to walk again. You can recover and not spend the rest of your life in the hospital. You can make it. You can succeed. But you must first affirm: *I deserve to succeed as much as anyone else.*

Every human being is born with one gift from God: The *privilege* of deserving to succeed. People aren't higher up the ladder than you are because they are more favored by God than you. You are as good as they are. And if you don't think so, then that's your problem. If so, I hope I can help you with it. You must affirm: *I deserve to succeed;* and *I have the ability to succeed.* Everyone has within himself latent, innate ability. It probably needs to be honed, educated, trained, and refined, but it can be done.

If you doubt your abilities, I can show you people who have learned to believe in their limited abilities enough to succeed far more than experts say they should. In a school for the severely mentally retarded in Mitchell, South Dakota, I've seen Down's Syndrome children with an average IQ of 36, writing sentences complete with verbs, nouns, and prepositions. There are vast, undeveloped areas in the most retarded mind. The reason more "handicapped" persons fail to develop their latent abilities is that other people don't believe they can. I've heard people say, "Don't waste your time on them." It's a tragic attitude.

I'll never forget Gail Bartosh. Her memory will always be an inspiration to me. She died just a few months ago and many of us miss her. Gail had Down's Syndrome. She spent the past twenty-six years in our church where her father had served as an elder. She believed in her possibilities and, the last ten years of her life, was a salaried, self-employed, self-sustaining person. She worked in the nursery and in our custodial department. People loved her!

Affirm. Anybody can amount to something if he will affirm himself and his abilities. Below, begin your own alphabet for winning.

A_____

_____

_____

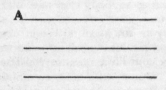

B Believe

Believe that somehow, some time, somewhere, through someone's help, you can achieve your heart's highest goal. All these words are important. The *A* stands for affirmation, belief in yourself, *B* is a belief that you can make it happen, but not by yourself. You can make it happen somewhere— but not necessarily where you are today. You can make it happen some way, even if you have to do things differently. You can make it happen some time—maybe not today, maybe not even this year. Perhaps this is the year of transition, during which you'll need to retool yourself intellectually and professionally with a new skill or a new trade.

No matter what your problem is, somehow, somewhere,

some way, some time, there is someone who has the key of wisdom to set you free.

B_____

_____

_____

 Commit

Commit yourself to a dream. You *affirm* you're created in the image of God, that you have latent abilities, that you deserve to succeed as much as anybody else, and after you begin to *believe* that somehow, some way, somewhere, some time, through someone, you can make it. When you are inspired with a dream, God has hit the ball into your court. Now you have to hit it back with a commitment. Most people fail right here on letter *C*, because, with every commitment, comes the risk of failure. Nothing devastates or holds people back more than the fear of failure.

A man who lost an election said to me, "Dr. Schuller, I feel like a total failure."

But I replied, "Anyone who announces his candidacy and campaigns for public office, only to lose, is not a total failure. In fact, nobody who tries to do something great but fails is a total failure. Why? Because he can always rest assured that he succeeded in life's most important battle—he defeated the fear of trying."

People who never declare their candidacy because they're afraid they'll lose, or people who never make an application because they're afraid they'll be turned down, or people who never try because they're sure they'll fail have lost the first battle. They have lost to fear. They have been knocked out before they even got in the ring.

Try. Go back to school, take a course. If you fail, at least you can have the pride of knowing you have conquered the fear of failure. You have won the one battle that knocks people out before they get started. *Make a commitment.*

 Dare

Dare to try. *Dare* to love. *Dare* to make a commitment. *Dare* to take a risk.

If you don't dare to take a risk, you'll never get ahead. You'll never solve your problems.

To laugh is to risk appearing the fool.

To weep is to risk appearing sentimental.

To reach for another is to risk involvement.

To expose your feelings is to risk exposing your true self.

To place your ideas, your dreams, before a crowd is to risk their loss.

To love is to risk not being loved in return.

To live is to risk dying.

To believe is to risk despair.

To try is to risk failure.

But risks must be taken, because the greatest hazard in life is to risk nothing.

The people who risk nothing, do nothing, have nothing, are nothing.

They may avoid suffering and sorrow, but they cannot learn, feel, change, grow, love, live.

Chained by their attitudes they are slaves; they have forfeited their freedom.

Only a person who risks is free.[1]

---

[1]*President's Newsletter*, Nov. 1982, Phi Delta Kappa, Bloomington, Indiana.

D_____

_____

_____

 Educate

Educate yourself. Don't be tempted, as many are, to take shortcuts, to avoid the hard years of serious study. The training may be a grind. But those who are too lazy to learn, who never gain the knowledge they could have, weaken their chances for success because knowledge is power. Ultimately, the knowledgeable person who has the right answers is the one who will impress the powerful people. So, get smart!

E_____

_____

_____

Find

Find the talent, the possibilities, the time, the money, and the way. There's a great Bible verse: "It is the glory of God to conceal a matter" (Prov. 25:2). God does not lay it all out in the open. No. The diamonds are deep in the earth. Pearls are concealed in oysters. The gold has to be carefully mined. Your real talent dwells deep down within you, and you may not have discovered it yet.

"It is the glory of God to conceal a matter." Why? Because the "matter" is much more exciting and meaningful when you have hunted for it and discovered it.

You have great possibilities hidden deep within yourself.

They wait to be discovered. They may be hidden at the core of a problem, or buried deep under a personal tragedy. Perhaps your greatest opportunity is wrapped up today in a blanket called "tough times." But find the positive power in the problem that you are facing. Find the help that is waiting for you, waiting to help you succeed.

An old Roman proverb says, "When there is no way, we will find one or build one." And a study of the building of the Roman roads confirms that they carried out that attitude.

G Give

A *giving* attitude is the secret to successful living. When you have an attitude of "I want what I want, when I want it," people can tell, and they are repelled. A lawyer friend says he has learned to smell a person's motives.

The secret of success is simple. Adele Scheele, the noted career guidance expert, said it, "If you're in a company, your aim should be to make that company more successful, more productive, more effective than it's ever been before." When you want to give something back over and beyond what you've earned in your paycheck, then you are going to be noticed.

There is a legend of a man who was lost in the desert, dying of thirst. He stumbled on until he came to an abandoned house. Outside the dilapidated, windowless, weather-beaten, deserted shack was a pump. He stumbled forward and began pumping furiously, but no water came from the well. Then he noticed a small jug with a cork at the top and a note written on the side: "You have to prime the pump with water, my friend. P.S. And fill the jug again before you leave." He pulled out the cork and saw that the jug was full of water.

Should he pour it down the pump? What if it didn't work? All of the water would be gone. If he drank the water from the jug, he could be sure he would not die of thirst. But to pour it down the rusty pump on the flimsy instruction written on the outside of the jug?

Something told him to follow the advice and choose the risky decision. He proceeded to pour the whole jug of water down the rusty old pump and furiously pumped up and down. Sure enough, the water gushed out! He had all he needed to drink. He filled the jug again, corked it, and added his own words beneath the instructions on the jug: "Believe me, it really works. You have to give it all away before you can get anything back."

The principle was well stated by the apostle Paul: "He who sows sparingly will also reap sparingly, and he who sows bountifully will also reap bountifully" (2 Cor. 9:6).

If you want to succeed, you have to "go for it" and give it all you've got.

The people who really succeed are the people who give extra effort and push themselves beyond their normal limits. There is a principle: "New powers are discovered every time you push yourself farther than you've ever gone before." There are deeper layers of energy, talent, and creativity within you, waiting to be tapped. No person ever fully discovers and develops all the potential within himself. Nobody ever drills the deepest well. Everybody—in his limited lifetime—falls short of uncovering the deeper talent and hidden possibility that lies far beneath the surface of his own consciousness.

G._____

_____

_____

Every
beginner
is a
*winner!**

**At least he won over inertia and procrastination and a
fear of starting.*

H Hope

Hope is holding on, praying expectantly. It's never giving up. It's never quitting.

A father once said to his boy, "Son, you gotta set a goal and never quit. Remember George Washington?"

The son said, "Yes."

"Jefferson?"

"Yes."

"Abraham Lincoln?"

"Yes."

"You know what they all had in common?"

"What?"

The father said, "They didn't quit. Remember Azador McIngle?"

The kid said, "No. Who was he?"

"See, you don't remember him! He quit!"

Hope. It is one of the most beautiful words in the New Testament. "And now abide faith, hope, love . . ." (1 Cor. 13:13).

At the International Psychiatric Congress in Madrid, Spain, which I attended, one of the main lectures was on the healing power of hope. Doctors, renowned psychiatrists from all over the world, gathered to discuss and agree that the single most important healing force is hope: hope of recovery, hope of loving and being loved, hope of making it, succeeding.

Carol Lovell is alive today because she had hope. Doctors attribute her survival after five bullet wounds in the head to hope, as much as anything else.

On September 4, 1981, Carol went to work early at the restaurant where she was employed as a bookkeeper. The building was empty, and she let herself in with her key. Soon Carol heard a knock at the door and recognized the man who stood there as a new custodian.

After she opened the door to him, he began slapping her around and demanded that she open the safe: "You're gonna be dead if you don't open the safe."

So, Carol opened the safe and gave him the money. *Now,* she thought, *he has what he's come for. He'll leave.*

But, the man was not done with Carol. He pulled her into the employee restroom, raped her, and shot her twice in the head.

Somehow, Carol maintained consciousness. Sure that her wounds would kill her, she prayed, "Lord, help me. I don't know how to die. I'm afraid. Give me the strength to die. Show me how." And then suddenly, she was able to pull herself to her feet. She thought, *I want to live; I don't want to die.* She ran to the front of the restaurant, and picked up the wrong phone, only to realize that she could not call out. She panicked when she realized her mistake, ran back to the office, and called a friend. She was asking her to call an ambulance when the man returned.

Seeing Carol, he shot her three more times. She fell to the floor, where she lay until the police and ambulance arrived.

She remained alert and amazingly calm as she described her attacker and informed the emergency attendants that she was wearing contact lenses. She was so calm, in fact, that the doctors felt freer to take time to determine the best way to remove the bullets from her head.

Her sister, Linda, arrived and began to fill her mind with hope and positive instructions. She told Carol, "You're going to be O.K. You're going to make it. Don't let your brain swell. Don't let your body bleed."

Amazingly, her brain never did swell, a common reaction to such a brain injury.

For weeks as Carol lay in intensive care, her sisters continued to feed her with positive thoughts and Scripture verses.

After six months of surgery, recovery, and therapy, Carol was walking and talking as she had before the accident. Her only residual difficulty after her attack has been an arm that tends to be uncooperative.

Carol's survival is incredible. She attributes her healing to hope. As she said to me, "Only prayer and positive thinking kept me going!"

Tough times never last, but tough people do. If you want to succeed, if you want to conquer, then *hope*—hold *o*n, praying *e*xpectantly!

H_____

_____

_____

Imagine

Possibility thinking is in actuality the exercise of dynamic, creative, sanctified *imagination*.

Sir Edmund Hillary, who attempted to scale Mount Everest, lost one of the members of his team in the failed effort. He returned to a hero's welcome in London, England, where a banquet held in his honor was attended by the lords and ladies and powerful people of the British Empire. Behind the speakers' platform were huge blown-up photographs of Mount Everest. When Hillary arose to receive the acclaim of the distinguished audience, he turned around and faced the mountain and said, "Mount Everest, you have defeated me. But I will return. And I will defeat you. *Because you can't get any bigger and I can.*"

I recently went through a rigorous training program for a long-distance run. In the five-mile stretch I covered every morning for two weeks was one hill that was really a toughie. The first morning, it almost forced me to walk. The second morning wasn't much easier. The third morning, I believed it was better. On the fifth morning as I approached it, I began to repeat a Bible verse: "every mountain and hill shall be made low" (Is. 40:4).

Then I recalled Hillary's comment, and I said to myself,

"God is going to strengthen me. God will make me bigger and tougher. That hill is a toughie. But *it can't get any tougher, but I can.*" It's amazing how easily I ran that hill, once I allowed my mind to become controlled by these positive thoughts.

Imagine solutions to your problem. Imagine yourself scaling your mountain. Imagine yourself crossing the finishing line.

I _____

_____

_____

J Junk

Junk the junk food of your mind. To keep hope alive, to be a creative imaginer, you have to throw out the tremendous load of junk food that we feed into our minds and emotions. What is emotional junk food? It's self-pity: "Why is this happening to me?" It's jealousy: "I don't think he's that good. He should have been laid off, instead of me." It's worry and anxiety. It's fear. Negative thoughts that stem from racial prejudices are also junk foods of the mind. People may have tried to put you down because of your color or national heritage, but you don't have to let them defeat you.

My friend Jester Hairston is an American treasure, an international institution. There isn't a high-school choir in the United States of America that hasn't sung one of the compositions or the arrangements of Jester Hairston. He is unquestionably the world's leading composer and arranger of Negro or Black spiritual music. I asked him, "What do you call it?"

He answered with a smile, "Negro, colored, Black, Afro-American folk songs."

"Jester, have you ever been the victim of racial prejudice?"

"I have been all my life. But I don't see any reason why I

should feature it. I have tried to outlive it. I can't just ignore it, but I have tried to outlive it. And I don't harbor the hatred of some people."

Jester has learned to junk the junk food of his mind. He has learned to outlive prejudice. Consequently, he has been a bridge-builder. His music, based in the roots of early Black American folk songs, has been sung by people the world over.

 Knock

Knock out depression, knock out discouragement, knock out all kinds of forecasts of gloom and doom. You may not be able to control everything that happens to you, but you can control how you will react. Even if the doctor has given you shattering news, you don't have to be knocked down. You can get up and fight. You can win—perhaps over the disease, but most certainly over the depression.

No one has fought more gallantly and won more graciously over the battle of cancer than beautiful Marguerite Piazza. This extraordinary woman sent me a cassette tape in which she told her story. I played her cassette one day while riding in my car. I was so moved that I had to pull over to the side of the road until she was finished.

It was in the peak of my career, performing in New York City, when I noticed a pink spot on my right cheek. I thought it was one of those 'zits,' as the kids say. I assumed it would go away. So I just put a little extra make-up on. But it didn't go away. Every time I was at the doctor for laryngitis or some other minor ailment I'd refer to my spot. They'd examine it, but always responded, "It's nothing. Don't worry about it." So I didn't. But it did not go away.

At this time, I was at a point in my life where I was known as the lady who had everything. I was one of the ten best-dressed women in the world. I was reported to be very beautiful. I was a star at the Metropolitan Opera. I had created a thing called "the act" for supper clubs. I was the first one to have dancers and all that kind of thing. *Variety* claimed it was the birth of a new form of show business. (Of course, today everybody does it.) I was married to a wonderful man who was a great, Southern gentleman and fun to live with. He had everything going for him.

Suddenly my world fell apart. Billy died of heart failure. Two weeks later, that spot on my cheek was diagnosed as melanoma, the worst form of skin cancer. It usually kills within seventeen months if it is not totally removed. They tried in three different operations to remove that melanoma from my cheek. They wanted to save my face because I was in show business. I was supposed to be beautiful, and you know show business is a business of beautiful people. If they did the radical surgery, I might end up like Scarface Lil.

The three operations weren't enough. The doctor said, "Marguerite, you must have radical surgery if you're going to live. You do have a choice. You can take a chance and decide not to have the radical. In so doing, you will keep your beauty, but you'll probably end up in a coffin. Or, you can let us do what we have to do—the radical. Then you'll have a possibility of living."

I was scheduled to sing that night. The house was sold out. The theater was packed with people who had come to hear me sing and see me dance.

What do you do at a time like that? Well, you do what you're paid to do. I was paid to lift people. So I prayed for strength. I went on. And each time there was a costume change between scenes or acts, and I took the costume off, hung it on the hanger, and got the new dress on, I hung my troubles on a hanger, left them in the closet, and went on stage. I sang my heart out and danced for all I was worth. The people loved it.

I did what I had to do on stage, and I did what I had to do for my children—I had the complete, radical surgery. Yes, I had six young children. I had no sisters or brothers. Now that their father was gone, I was all that they had. So, I promised the Lord if He would just let me live so I could take care of my children, that I'd never complain.

I went through the radical. They removed my entire right cheek, all the glands in my neck, the carotid artery, and the muscle in my right shoulder. I was the worst-looking sight you'd ever see in your whole life.

I came home. I showed the children what had happened, and I explained to them that I was going to be O.K. They were still very shaken from the recent death of their father. Yes, sir, I was going to be O.K.! I didn't know if I could go back into show business or go back into supper clubs. It takes a lot of fortitude, and I didn't know if everybody would accept me with this scarred face.

I had ten or eleven plastic surgeries to remove the scars. I'm singing again. I'm performing for my Lord, and He has pleased me. He has brought a wonderful man into my life who has become my husband and has been a great father to my children.

I liken my experience to that of a child who is totally absorbed in something. My son Gregory would be reading a book or watching the tube and I'd say, "Gregory, come here." He wouldn't seem to hear me. I once asked the doctor, "Do you think that child is deaf?"

He said, "No, of course not. He has a great sense of concentration. But, Marguerite, if you want his attention, go up to him and shake him a little bit. He'll look at you. Then tell him what you want."

That's the way it was with me and the Lord. He needed my attention. I wasn't doing exactly what He wanted me to do yet. So He shook me—with a second cancer. I couldn't believe it. But there it was. I went through seventy-two hours of radiation and another operation. That is when I learned that stress can kill you. It almost killed me because I was filled with stress. Stress was controlling me.

If there's anything I've learned through all of this, it's that the mind is extremely important. What you focus your thoughts on will be manifested in your outer life. If you think stress and fear, they will manifest in your life. And if you think love and understanding, they will also manifest and bring to you all of the things that God wants you to have.

Do as Marguerite did—knock out depression, discouragement, forecasts of gloom and doom. Take control of your life and your future by knocking out all negativity.

K_____

_____

_____

 Laugh

You must keep a sense of humor and be able to *laugh* at yourself. Have you heard the story of Oral Roberts, Billy Graham, and Robert Schuller? The story goes that they all died earlier than planned. Peter met them at the gate: "I'm sorry, guys. Your rooms aren't ready yet. You'll have to wait downstairs in hell until your room is ready."

Before long, Satan called and said, "Peter, hurry up and get these guys out of here. Oral Roberts is healing the sick. Billy Graham's saving all the souls, and Robert Schuller's raising money to air-condition the place!"

Believe me, you can't be a successful possibility thinker unless you can laugh at yourself and laugh at life's difficulties. If you keep your sense of humor and laugh, then you'll be able to love. I really don't think it's possible to love until you laugh first. People who try to love before they laugh take themselves too seriously.

There are too many counterfeit forms of love and too many people who say, "I love you because I need you," or "I love you because I want you." Such possessive forms of love are not real. They seek to *get* something from the other person instead of *giving* something. When you laugh, you can love, because then you're loving people because they need you and the joy you can bring to their life.

M Make it happen

You can make it happen when you *manage*, because possibility thinking is really another label for dynamic mental management. You make it happen.

Colonel Norman Vaughan is a man who has led one of the most exciting lives imaginable. He made it happen. He wanted adventure so he went after it.

The son of a financially capable father, Vaughan was a sophomore at Harvard when he picked up a paper and read: "Byrd to the South Pole." He felt destined to go. Something said to him, "Get going. Close your books." So he did. The next day he was at Admiral Byrd's house.

Norman rang the doorbell. The maid came, but wouldn't let him past the door. She said that only those who had an appointment could see Commander Byrd.

He was nothing but a college kid. After a moment of disappointment he turned and walked down the steps to the sidewalk. When he hit the sidewalk, he quickened his pace and almost ran to the newspaper office to see the man who had written the piece on Admiral Byrd. He asked the reporter to intercede for him and relay his hopes to Admiral Byrd.

It worked. Commander Byrd accepted his proposal.

So Norman left Harvard immediately. He went to where Admiral Byrd was assembling his dogs, and he devoted a year to the commander's work, sleeping on the ground in a tent, winter and summer. In order to eat, he volunteered to be a waiter at the nearest inn, in exchange for leftover food.

Admiral Byrd reviewed Norman's efforts and decided to take him on the expedition.

Since he had had experience driving dogsleds, Norman

was classified as one of the five professional dogsled drivers. They took ninety-seven dogs, ten teams, to unload the two ships. The entire expedition was one of the most exciting events in which anyone could ever participate. Norman was there because he made it happen. Admiral Byrd did not come to him. Norman's father did not approve of his quick departure from Harvard, so he did not finance Norman's venture. Norman wanted to make it—and he did. He made it happen!

He told me, "The most challenging moment of the whole expedition was when Admiral Byrd asked me if I could pull a Ford Tri-Motor from the ship out to Little America, a distance of nine miles. I said that I didn't know but that I'd try. So we put a long hawser from the ship out across the snow toward Little America. I brought all ninety-seven dogs with the various teams together in front of that airplane. We harnessed the dogs to that hawser and tried to get them started.

"In order to start a heavy load, you lift the gang line, and drop it. Well, lifting the gang line for ninety-seven dogs took two or three other men with me. We lifted it and let it go. And supposedly, when there was a slack in the line, all the dogs would pull. We worked an hour and a half, until suddenly, through no particular reason any of us could ever detect, the ship moved. When it moved, all ninety-seven dogs began to pull. We didn't stop until we hit Little America. We jogged along in front of that airplane with our dogs. And that's the largest sled dog team that was ever harnessed up until that time."

Do you want excitement? Do you want your dream to come true? Then make it happen!

M_____

_____

_____

N Negotiate

If you want to get from *A* to *Z* in the Alphabet for Action for Possibility Thinkers you have to be able to *negotiate*, to compromise. You can't have your way all the time.

When we started in the drive-in theater twenty-five years ago, I began to dream of a church of my own. My first dream was for a forty-acre plot. However, when a forty-acre parcel became available, we couldn't afford it. So, I negotiated, I compromised, and I decided that we *actually* needed only ten acres. That's all we bought. Later on, we added another ten acres. Better half a loaf than none!

Scale down, if necessary. Don't be embarrassed. It's better to change plans while the ship is in port than to save face, only to sink in the middle of the ocean. Be willing to start smaller and add to your plans as you grow.

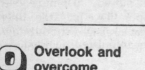

O Overlook and overcome

If you've made it to *O* you'll have been successful enough to know that you can't succeed without a team. You can't get very far without some kind of organization. That means that you will have to work with people. They're not going to be perfect; there will be times when they will let you down. They're going to make mistakes, and if you demand perfection from them, you're going to be hard to work for. The good people will leave. Therefore you have to overlook your own and other people's imperfections. When you overlook, you'll be able to overcome.

Do you have a problem that is so big that you don't know

how to handle it? Then maybe you need to overlook and look over.

What do I mean by "look over"? Let me explain it with a story.

One day a pastor went walking in the country and saw a cow looking over the wall. As he stood looking at the cow, he was approached by a member of his church who asked him, "Is something wrong, pastor?"

He replied, "Well, I'm having troubles."

The farmer said, "Pastor, look at the cow. What's that cow doing?"

"She's looking over the wall."

The farmer said, "Why do you think she's looking over the wall?"

"Oh, I don't know."

"She's looking over the wall because she can't see *through* it."

I must tell you that during my twenty-seven years in this church, I have come up against some walls I couldn't see through.

I've come to the conclusion that there are lots of problems that can't be solved. In my first book, *Move Ahead With Possibility Thinking*, there was a chapter entitled, "There's a Solution to Every Problem." I don't believe that any more. I think there are some problems that can't be solved. However, every problem can be overcome, manipulated, molded.

O_____

_____

_____

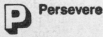

Persevere

Persevere; don't give up. Tough times never last, but tough people do.

You may have heard of Kathy Miller. Millions saw her story

when it was made into a movie for television. But, I want to share it with you because if anyone has persevered over tough times, it has been Kathy Miller.

When Kathy was thirteen, going on fourteen, she was struck by a car. This beautiful, bubbly, popular young woman, who had once been a runner, was suddenly motionless and silent. She lay in a coma, week after week without any sign of life.

Eleven weeks after the accident, Kathy regained consciousness, only to face her toughest battle. The accident had left her brain-damaged. She was like a baby who had to learn to eat, drink, walk, and talk. And when she finally got to the point where she was able to try to resume her life, she was bitterly disappointed.

By then her friends were in high school. They had continued to grow and mature, while Kathy had suffered a major setback. She had reverted to childhood, and had lost weight to the point where she weighed only about fifty pounds. She was skin and bones, and her speech and body motions were far from normal. When she compared herself to others, she fell short. Nobody could relate to her. It was a tough time for her.

But Kathy had a dream that kept her going. Her dream was to run in the North Banks 10,000 meter run.

Barely able to walk, running such an arduous race seemed absurd. But Kathy was determined. She trained vigorously, building her body for the race.

She wanted to run the course. Finishing would be like winning for Kathy.

On the day of the race, all of the other runners sprinted far ahead of her. Before long, she couldn't see them. All alone she ran, step after step, her body aching, her heart pounding, her lungs burning. Often she fell, sprawling face down onto the pavement. But she picked herself up, put one crippled foot a few inches ahead of the other, and dragged her other leg up to meet the foot. She repeated this process countless times. As she persevered, the blocks stretched into miles. The sun had risen high in the sky and was beginning to descend as Kathy neared the last stretch of her run. Just as she began to fear she couldn't continue, that she would have to quit, she saw some friends from high school who had felt uneasy around Kathy's disabilities. Now they were cheering her on: "Go, Kathy! Keep going! You're doing great!"

Kathy made it. She finished the race. She's a winner. In fact, she received the Philadelphia Sportswriters' Award as the most courageous athlete in America and the International Award for Valor.

She graduated from high school with honors—straight A's.

I said recently to Kathy, "You're a winner. You have persevered. But tell me, what do you say to people who lose, even after they've given it all they have?"

She replied, "To me, winning is not necessarily being first or best at something. When you give it all you've got, then you win. Winning to me is just that: Giving what you've got for the Lord, just coming through whatever trial you face."

I asked her another question: "What do you say to someone who has problems, who's really hurting?"

"My word to them would be to just hang in there and keep plugging at it. Know that you're winning through Christ and that He's there and He'll help in His perfect timing!"

Persevere. It's a very important word in our alphabet for action.

 Quit

Quit complaining because life isn't as nice as you want it. Look at what you have left, never at what you've lost. Quit remembering all of those negative, haunting memories.

This past week, I called on a dear friend of mine, Mrs. Putnam. She lives in Cleveland on the shores of Lake Erie. Not too long ago, at eighty-three, she fell and broke her hip. She said to me from her chair, "I was unconscious for three days; they thought I wouldn't live, but I did." Then she looked at me and said, "Dr. Schuller, how do you stay happy all the time?"

I said, "Well, for one thing I decided long ago to throw out all of the excess baggage of my mind. By that I mean the baggage of bad memories. Throw it out."

"How do you do that?"

Before I answered her, I looked at a picture of her deceased husband, hanging on the wall. He was a fantastic man, one of the great American lords of industry. I also noticed the picture of her son in uniform, killed in World War II. Now here she was, unable to walk. She repeated her question, "How do you unload the bad memories? How do you rid them from your life?"

I said, "Mrs. Putnam, can you stand?"

She said, "Oh, I think so."

I stretched out my hands. She took the blanket off her knees, and took hold of my hands. I held her tightly above the elbows and slowly led her until she was four feet from the window. And I asked, "What do you see?"

She said, "I see Lake Erie."

"I'll bet when you were younger you used to stand here on the lawn and throw a stone and you'd watch it fly into the lake."

She said, "Oh, yes, but I haven't done that for many years."

"Did you know that your mind can throw a bad thought a lot farther than your arm has ever thrown a stone? Mrs. Putnam, any time an unpleasant memory or any unpleasant feeling or a negative thought comes into your brain, I want you to stand, if not physically, at least mentally, right here and look through the window. With your mind, throw that thought through the glass until it sinks deep into the lake. Then I want you to sit down and read these lines." And I handed her a piece of paper on which I had just scrawled four lines from an anonymous author:

> I shut the door on yesterday
> and threw the key away.
> Tomorrow has no fears for me
> Since I have found today.

She said, "I can do it!"
So can you if you'll quit complaining!

Q——————————

—————————————

—————————————

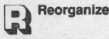 **Reorganize**

If you haven't yet succeeded, then you have to say, "I need to *reorganize*." When you fail, you will need to reorganize. And when you succeed you will need to reorganize.

Whether you've failed or succeeded, chances are, there are parts of your life that need reorganization. The only person who doesn't have to reorganize constantly is the person for whom life and business has become static. Anybody whose life is static is dead.

I've been reorganizing the past month. I took a few days off with my wife and we prayed. I asked these questions, to myself, to God, to my wife:

1. Who am I?
2. Where have I come from?
3. How did I get here?
4. Where do I want to go?
5. How can I get there?

I knew who I was last month, and last year, but I'm constantly changing. I need to frequently reevaluate who I am and where I am going. And right now I'm reorganizing my life around the answers to those questions.

A few years ago the doctor told my wife that she had a cancerous tumor in her breast. Just before the surgery, she called her doctor and me to her bedside and said, "After the surgery I want to know what the score is. If cancer has spread through my body, and I have only twelve months to live, I want to know right away, because there are two things I want to do before I die." We agreed. However, thank God, her surgery was successful. We believe she's permanently cured. But about a year or two ago, I remembered what she had told me just before her surgery. I asked her, "Honey, do you remember what you said to me just before surgery? What are the two things you wanted to do?"

She said, "Number one, I wanted to organize all my closets and drawers. I didn't want to be dead and have other people go through the drawers and closets and say, 'Boy, what a mess!' The second thing I wanted to do was write a personal letter to each of my children."

Reorganize. Times change. You may have to change your whole corporate structure. You may have to abolish some departments. Sometimes you have to go back to get on the right track. Maybe you need to advance. Perhaps you need to retreat or regroup. Maybe you need to scale your operation up or down, maybe even close down. Whatever your situation is, chances are that you need to reorganize.

R_____

_____

_____

 Share

God can do tremendous things through the person who doesn't care who gets the credit and is willing to *share* the credit, *share* the power, and *share* the glory.

More than one company has been successful, only to reach a certain leveling-off period where it began to die. The reason? The guy who started and developed the business reached a point where he couldn't handle all the administration, but he couldn't bring himself to delegate it to others. Some people are afraid to delegate because they think no one else can do as good a job as they.

I've gone through that. But I came to this conclusion. It's better to let somebody else do a worse job than I would do, than not have it get done at all. The surprising thing is that, more often than not, they do a better job of it than I would have done!

Share your feelings and share your gratitude. Say "Thank you" to the people who helped make it happen. At the point of success, don't forget to share appreciation. I don't forget the fact that I'm totally dependent upon friends and members of the church who keep the ministry going. Share your appreciation by using that powerful word, "Thanks."

In a cynical moment of interviewing, a newspaper reporter said to Rudyard Kipling, "Mr. Kipling, I just read that somebody calculated that the money you make from your writings amounts to over one hundred dollars a word." Mr. Kipling raised his eyebrows and said, "Really? I wasn't aware of that." Then the reporter said, "Here's a hundred-dollar bill, Kipling. Give me one of your hundred-dollar words."

Kipling looked at the hundred dollar bill, finally took it, quietly folded it up, and said, "Thanks." Then he turned and walked away.

S_____

_____

_____

T Trade-off

When you have begun to reorganize and share, then you will have to get ready to *trade-off*. That means that you will have to decide what you will give up in order to keep what you've got.

A minister friend of mine who played golf told his wife how important it was. He said, "It's good for my work. I meet important men and women on the golf course." But one day as he was heading for the car with his clubs, his little four-year-old boy, watching at the screen door, said, "Daddy, can I go with you?"

The minister said, "Sorry, son, you can't go golfing with me." The little boy's eyes filled with tears. The father waved, started the car, and drove off. He had only gone about two blocks when he turned around, drove back, rushed into the house, swept his son in his arms, and said, "Hey, buddy, would you rather go fishing?" At that point, he made a great trade-off, exchanging one human priority for a better one.

The other day I was in Paul Harvey's studio in Chicago as he was making his broadcast. Paul said, "It's time for me to go on the air; but why don't you join me in the studio? It's live, you know." I went in the studio. He closed the door. The red light was blinking. He cleared his throat. "Good morning, Americans, this is Paul Harvey speaking." And away he went. He said, "I happen to know somebody, a minister, who, I'm told, chose to fail in order that he could choose to succeed. Is that right, Robert Schuller?"

I said, "Right, Paul Harvey. I chose to fail at golf, because I wanted to succeed as a father. Yes, I traded-off my hobby of playing golf in favor of my desire to be a successful dad." At this time, maybe you have to trade-off power for peace, dollars for joy, and glory for the greater joy of seeing other people grow.

T_____

_____

_____

The me
I see...
is the
me I'll be!

Unlock

Unlock some human values you never experienced before—faith, hope, and love. Let these values be the driving force propelling you toward true success. What is success? It is being in a position to help others who are hurting.

I know of no man who is more successful than Dr. Howard House.

If you were to ask medical doctors around the world to name those doctors that rank in the highest category of specialists concerning surgery and diseases of the ear, the first to be named would be Dr. Howard P. House of Los Angeles. He is president of a world-renowned, unexcelled research center for the development of solutions to hearing problems.

I recently had the honor of meeting this remarkable man. I was immediately impressed by the love and concern he had for the people he helps. He told me he first decided to become a doctor when he announced to his father, a renowned dentist, that he would follow in his footsteps.

His father surprised him, however, by responding, "If I had it to do over again, I would go to medical school and then into dentistry, because you can't divorce the teeth from the rest of the body."

Years later, when Howard finished medical training, he apologized to his father for going into medicine instead of dentistry. His father replied, "Do you remember that evening when I suggested you go into medicine instead of dentistry? Why do you think I did that? Because medicine is a much broader field. It offers many more opportunities for research and development and care of people."

Concern for people. This is what motivated Dr. House. This is what spurred him to learn all he could. At the close of his medical education, as Howard was being drawn towards a specialty in eyes, ears, nose, and throat, his father asked him, "Howard, is there anyone in this country that knows more about eyes, ears, noses, and throats than you do?"

Howard had to say, "Of course."

[222]

His father said, "There will never be a better time than now to visit each one of those doctors and see what motivated him, what made him the man he is today." So in 1937 he set out for Stockholm, Sweden, to see for the very first time a new operation to restore hearing performed by a Professor Homgren. When Howard House saw this remarkable surgery, he decided at that moment that it's much more important to create a sense of hearing for a person who is hard-of-hearing than to give him a better-looking nose.

Since then he has performed more than thirty-two thousand ear surgeries. And along with his brother Bill, he has developed an implant of minute wires that restores hearing after otoschlerosis, a progressive hearing-loss disease.

They have also developed the cochlear implant, little electrodes in the inner ear that bring hearing to deaf children.

He has placed implants in more than two hundred such patients, the first in 1968. He recalled to me the joy he felt recently when, for the first time, he did an implant on a three-year-old child: "Just to watch this child delight with hearing for the first time, sounds lost because of meningitis when she was a year and a half old! She loves the sounds! She loves to hear the sound of her feet as she walks on the floor. It brings tears to all of our eyes when we see this little girl's response."

Literally thousands of doctors come from around the world to the House Institute to learn the techniques of the House brothers.

"A brilliant man," you say. Yes, you are right. Smarter than you? I doubt it. I've seen his college transcripts. Are you ready for this? At the end of his first year in college he had a 2.0 grade-point average. He had mostly D's, including a D in chemistry. He even had one F. The following year, he didn't do any better. In fact, he did worse. He ended up with a 1.35 grade-point average. The third year, he perked up and got all the way up to a 2.2. At that point, Howard went to see Dean McKibben at the University of Southern California and told him he was interested in going into medicine. The dean said, "You're not serious."

But he did tell Howard that if he worked hard and came back the next year with a better grade, he'd have a place for him. So Howard dropped a number of extracurricular activities. His grades improved. Thanks to Dean McKibben, he entered medical school.

Today, more than thirty-two thousand people have discovered the glory of sound thanks to a caring, dedicated man— Dr. Howard House—but only because he unlocked the love and faith in his heart and let them be the driving force of his life.

U_____

_____

_____

V Visualize

Visualize the dream before you. Don't ever lose the vision. When you lose the vision, you're dead. Where there are no dreams, people perish.

A young lad came to college as a freshman and checked into his room. The first thing he did was hammer a big brass letter *V* on his door. Everybody asked him what it was for, but he wouldn't tell them. He kept it polished, and it was always the first thing put up in his room as he moved from dorm to dorm. Finally he graduated and at the commencement exercise, his name was announced as valedictorian. When he walked across the stage, there in his left hand was his polished brass letter *V*.

Set new goals. Believe you can reach them. Visualize defeat and you will be defeated. Visualize ultimate success, and you will achieve it! *What you see is what you'll be.*

I recently spoke at a convention of two thousand salespersons employed by an obviously very successful direct sales business woman. The leader's father, who was a university graduate, was understandably disappointed when she dropped out of high school. As a result of his disappointment, this woman developed a terribly negative self-image. After years of feeling like a flop and a failure, she was introduced to possibility thinking. As a result she made a trip to California and worshiped in the Crystal Cathedral.

Soon after, she learned of a good, useful product that people needed. She believed in it. Friends encouraged her to market this product and become a salesperson. "But," she said, "I can't be a salesperson. I don't know anything about it. And besides I'm not very smart. I never finished school." But before she threw the idea away for good, she remembered these words: "With God all things are possible." She gave it a try. She succeeded, and a few days ago I spoke to two thousand of her employees.

Success all starts in your head, and every person has the freedom to choose to be a success or not. It's that simple: Choose to succeed. See yourself as a successful person, and you will be a successful person.

Visualize. *The me I see is the me I'll be.* You can be anything or anyone you want to be if you can learn to believe in yourself.

It is true that God gives different abilities and different gifts to different people, but, ultimately, success doesn't come through special abilities. You can look at people in your profession who are higher up the ladder than you are. You know that you are as talented as they. Conversely, you can look down the ladder only to see a crowd of equally talented people nipping at your heels.

Neither success nor self-esteem necessarily comes through *talent.* Nor do they necessarily come through *territory.* Some people surmise that they would find success if they lived in a particular town or state. Although it is easier to succeed in America than in any other country, merely living in America does not guarantee success.

I was in Hong Kong not long after the Communist takeover, when the Chinese poured onto that island. I was in Berlin shortly after the Wall went up to keep people rushing from the East to the West. Today, people are fleeing to America. Why? Because life is easier in America than in any other country. But, ultimately, success doesn't come from where you are but from the way you think! It comes from visualizing your dream. That's why possibility thinkers who may not have the talent, the territory, or the training achieve the impossible. They go through tough times and they survive. Why? Because they believe in themselves. They feel that they have as much right as anyone else to be happy and to be successful.

You won't find real success or self-worth through the right *ties*, nor will you find it in mere undeveloped *talent*, nor in living in the right town, community, country, or *territory*. You won't necessarily find success or self-esteem through *training* either.

Success comes from visualizing yourself the way you want to be. Do you think you are terrific? You are! You just have to believe in yourself. I probably won't be able to convince you of it, for persons can't be convinced they are beautiful if they don't think they're beautiful.

I recall every one of my four daughters, at least once in their lives, when they got a new haircut or permanent, asking me, "How does it look?" I would say, "It looks great." But in their uncertainty they replied, "Oh, I don't think it does. I bet it doesn't look good at all!"

Even though I thought it looked great and I told them so, they remained unconvinced. The same is true for you. I can convince you of your talents, but I can't convince you of what you can accomplish in life. Only one person can convince you . . . God. The way you think about yourself depends on the way you think about God. I call it possibility thinking. It's the secret of success! Why is it so powerful? It's powerful because of what it does for you. It tells you that you are potentially as smart and inherently successful as any other person.

How do you visualize yourself? *The me I see is the me I'll be.* I want you to ask yourself this question: "What new goals would I set for myself, if I could be sure that I would succeed?" Think about it. Pray about it. And get ready to act on it.

Paul said it: "I can do all things through Christ who strengthens me" (Phil. 4:13). Where do I get my dreams? Why, from Jesus Christ. God put you in this world. He has a dream for you. Open up to His dream and see yourself as He sees you. "As he [man, woman, or child] thinks in his heart, so is he" (Prov. 23:7).

I shall never forget him. I met him this past year at a conference. He was only twenty-two years of age, but one of the top salespersons. The young man had been diagnosed a few years earlier with cystic fibrosis. After his fatal disease was discovered, nobody would hire him. He was told, "You won't live long enough to make it worthwhile."

His father and mother were poor. They could hardly pay the medical bills.

He thought, *I may be sick; I may be dying; but I can still do something. It would be much better to accomplish something great than to just sit here and wait to die.* So he accepted an invitation to join a direct sales business. He was a terrific salesman, because, as he said, "I don't have long to live, so if I want to break any records, I'd better do it in a hurry."

When I saw him, he was wearing a Hawaiian shirt. He said, "Do you know why I'm wearing this shirt? After I made enough money to put a savings account aside to take care of my funeral expenses, I gave some of the rest to the Lord, and I decided to take my mother and father to Hawaii. We just got back. We had a wonderful time!" He was only skin and bones under the Hawaiian T-shirt. He's no longer with us. But, boy, he's really alive now, for he knew the Lord.

The me I see is the me I'll be.

How do you see yourself?

There are too many people today who are suffering from an inferiority complex. There are several factors in our society that could contribute to it. Too many rely on these factors as excuses for not being all that they could be. Others are hurt and they say, "What's the point of trying, just to get knocked down again?"

But some people have learned to rise above the blows that life has dealt them. They discover that they are somebody special, regardless of what others say or how they are treated. They keep proving the truth of this book. *Tough times never last, but tough people do!*

I think of the woman who emigrated from Mexico to the United States with her husband and children. On their way to "paradise," at the border in El Paso, Texas, her husband deserted her, leaving her stranded with the children. A divorcee, twenty-two years of age with two kids, she was poverty-stricken. With the few dollars in her pocket, she bought bus tickets to California. There she was sure she could find work. She did find a job—an awful job, working from midnight until six o'clock in the morning, making tacos. She earned only a few dollars, but she ate meagerly and saved a dime from every dollar she earned.

Why did she save? She saved because she was visualizing a dream—she wanted to own a taco shop. One day she took the few dollars she'd managed to save, went to a banker, and said, "There's a little place I'd like to buy. If you'd loan me a few thousand dollars, I can have my own taco shop."

The banker, impressed by her, decided to take a chance and loaned her the money. She was twenty-five years old and the owner of a little taco shop. She worked hard at it, and eventually, she expanded and expanded until today, fifteen years later, she has the largest wholesale business of Mexican products in America. She went on to become the treasurer of the United States. Her name is Ramona Banuelos.

She was asked, "What's the biggest problem facing your people in America today?"

She replied, "Children are growing up in America thinking they are inferior. I'll never forget the day my little daughter came home from school and said, 'Mama, am I Spanish or Mexican?' When I said, 'You're Mexican,' her face dropped. She was so depressed. She said, 'I wish I were Spanish.' When I wanted to know why it mattered, she answered, 'Because the Spanish people are very smart and Mexicans aren't.'"

Ramona Banuelos said, "That's not true! Mexicans are not inferior!" To prove her point, she took her children to Mexico, and she showed them the ruins of the Aztec temples, telling them, "These were built by Mexicans not Spaniards." She showed them the wide boulevards and the great architecture. "These were built by the Aztecs; that's the blood you have in you. Be proud you are a Mexican—you have good blood in you!"

You are somebody. You bet you are. No matter what your race, no matter what your color, no matter what your ethnic background, you are the child of a survivor! That's right! If you trace your roots to Africa, Europe, Mexico, or Malaysia, or wherever, you will find times of great suffering in the history of your people.

Success doesn't come through the ways you may think it comes, it comes through the way you think! Think positively. Visualize success!

V_____

_____

_____

W Work

There is no substitute for *work*.

The other night, my wife and I took the world famous pianist, Roger Williams, to dinner in appreciation for the times he has donated his talents to our ministry. At ten o'clock, he said, "Well, I really have to go. I must get to work."

"Work? At this time?"

"Yes, it's a rehearsal," he said. "I will go home and rehearse from ten o'clock till about two o'clock. I'll sleep for about three or four hours, and then I'll get up and rehearse for another two hours."

I asked, "Do you do that every day?"

He said, "Oh, yes, every day."

The people at the top of the ladder work harder than anyone else. Why? Because they have gotten into the habit of working hard. There is no substitute for it. Success is spelled w-o-r-k.

If you ever flunked a college course, it wasn't because you weren't smart enough. You just didn't apply yourself. The difference in IQ isn't that significant on a college level; the difference is in application.

A little boy in patched overalls asked a rich general contractor in fancy clothes, observing the skyscraper rising under his supervision, "How can I be rich like you when I grow up?"

The tough old construction man looked at the little fellow and, using the crusty language of one who had come up from the soil of labor, said, "Buy a red shirt, son, and work like hell."

The startled little boy obviously didn't understand what the older man was telling him. The man pointed to the workmen crawling around several stories of the open steel framework of the rising skyscraper and said to the boy, "Look at those men working there. They all work for me. I don't know them by name. I've never met some of them. But look at that fellow in the red shirt. Everybody else is wearing blue. I've noticed that the man in red works harder than anyone else. He comes in every morning, just a bit earlier than anybody else. He seems to work faster than anybody else. He is the last one to clock off the job. He stands out from the crowd because he wears that red shirt every day. I'm about to go over there and ask him to be my supervisor. From there, I suspect he is going to rise to the top and maybe become one of my vice presidents.

"That's how I made it, son. I decided to work a little harder and a little better than anybody else on the job. And if I wore blue overalls, nobody would ever notice me. So I always wore a striped shirt. I worked harder. I stood out from the crowd. I was noticed. I got the promotions. I saved my money. And that's how I got where I am today."

W_____

_____

_____

X X-ray

If you're pursuing a job, if you're on your way toward a goal, if you've got a dream, and you've gotten this far, then it's high time you stopped once more and *x-rayed* your deepest motives.

There are people who have high moral and ethical integrity in their businesses. If you took a moral, spiritual, and an ethical x-ray of one of these people, put it up on the board, and flipped the light on, you'd say, "Wow, he's in great shape!" However, if you saw your own x-ray, you might not like what you see. You've been making a lot of money; that's great. I tell people, "Make all the money you can legally. Save all you can. Then give all you can. But if dollars become an end in themselves, then you're in trouble."

You need to ask yourself, first, "What do I really want to accomplish?" Then ask yourself, "If I continue the way I am, will I get to where I really want to go?" Then you ask a third question: "If I get there, will I be happy? And will that really fulfill me at my deepest level?" That's what you call x-ray.

X_____

_____

_____

Y Yield

In a great verse from the Book of Romans, Paul said, "Yield yourselves unto God" (Rom. 6:13 KJV). When it's all said and done, you must have done this long before you come to the Z of the alphabet for action.

By the time you've asked, "Where have I come from; what do I want; where am I going; will I be happy if I get there?," then you must be ready to yield it all to God. By the time you get through the x-ray, you may find out that you've been running after the world, but neglecting your own soul. Jesus said it: "For what will it profit a man if he gains the whole world, and loses his own soul?" (Mark 8:36).

Yield yourself to God, because you're very close to the Z, and the Z is the end.

The late Senator Hubert Humphrey said to me, shortly before he died, that he wanted to come to the end of his life with pride behind him, love around him, and hope ahead of him. How will you come to your end? What will it be like? After life, what do you take with you? If you leave it behind, who gets it?

I met a man on a plane. I did not recognize his face, though his name is a household word. He said, "Dr. Schuller, I want to tell you—I like you on television."

I said, "Thank you."

"My wife and my mother never miss you either."

"Thank you."

He said, "My name is Bear Bryant."

I said, "It's always super to meet a great Christian."

He protested, "I'm not sure I am a Christian!"

I asked, "Well, don't you believe in Jesus?"

"Yeah, I believe in Jesus, sure."

"Why do you think you're not a Christian?"

"Well," he said, "first of all, I don't have the feeling. These born-again Christians have a feeling that I don't think I have.

I've talked to Billy Graham, I've talked to Oral Roberts, and I'm talking to you. I still don't have that feeling.

"And a second thing bothers me," he said. "There are some things in the Bible I just cannot understand. It says in the Bible that this prophet sent some bears to eat up some little kids. I don't think God would want a bear to eat up little kids."

I said, "What else?"

He said, "The third thing is, I do some things I shouldn't do. Like smoking; I shouldn't smoke if I am a Christian."

I said, "Coach, I want to be your coach on the spiritual plane. A Christian is not somebody who understands and believes in every word in the Bible. That's not the definition of a Christian. When you get to heaven, God isn't going to ask, 'Do you believe in every word in the Bible?' That's not the judgment. I think Christians all believe the Bible is the Word of God, but there may be some things they have difficulty understanding. You're not saved by the Book, you're saved by the blood.

"Also, Christianity isn't a feeling, it is a faith. I'd have to agree with you— I've never had a moment when I would say I was 'born again' in the sense that one day was black and the next day, white. I never had that. Christianity is faith, not feeling.

"Finally, being a Christian is surely not a matter of being a perfect person. I have my sins, too. I'm not perfect."

He said, "I wish I knew that, if the end were to come, I would go to heaven."

I said, "Well, I can help you there."

I took a piece of paper, and I wrote Jesus' promise: "The one who comes to me I will by no means cast out" (John 6:37).

I said, "Look at that, coach. That's a promise Jesus made. I know that when my end comes, I will step into the sunshine and not into the darkness. There will be eternal daylight, not eternal darkness, for me. I believe in heaven. If I believe in a yes, there's got to be a no. If I believe in light, there's got to be darkness. If I believe in heaven, there has to be a hell.

"Not everybody's going to heaven, coach. When I go there, I'm going to be carrying in my hand and my heart this promise of Jesus: 'The one who comes to me I will by no means cast out.'

"Jesus is my Friend. He would never turn a friend away. Do you believe that?"

He said, "Yes, sir."

I drew a straight line and dated it. I said, "O.K., coach, sign it."

He looked at the paper and said, "Well, I don't know if I can be sure if I should sign that or not today."

I said, "*I* can't be sure that this plane will land, either."

He said, "I'll sign it!"

Yield your life and your problems to God. Once you've given God control of your life, it won't be free from difficulty. God has not promised that our skies will always be blue, but He has promised to see us through.

My daughter Sheila gave her life to God years ago. Her life has been full—a fulfilling career, a loving husband, and two delightful boys, Jason, two, and Christopher, three months.

Yet her life had not been free from tough times. Last Saturday, the phone rang as we were busy preparing for my daughter Carol's birthday party. I answered the phone. It was Sheila.

"Dad, I'm here at Children's Hospital. It's Christopher. They say he has asthma, a double ear infection, and spinal meningitis. They did a spinal tap. It's positive. There are some cells in the spinal fluid." Then she broke down: "Pray for my baby."

Sheila and her husband, Jim, followed the nurse down the hospital corridor. She held her hot little baby close to her. When she glanced up, she saw to her surprise, written on the doors, "Intensive Care Unit." They stepped into a world of machines and individual rooms with windows. Through them, they could see other babies, some in oxygen tents, all hooked up to monitors.

The nurse took Sheila's baby from her, undressed him, hooked him up to monitors, and placed him in a steel crib.

Then the doctors came in, hovered over him, and examined him thoroughly.

The primary doctor said, "Mr. and Mrs. Coleman, we will be starting an IV with medication for the asthma and antibiotics for the infection and meningitis. My suggestion to you is to go home and get some rest. Your baby will need you more tomorrow than today."

So Jim and Sheila went home, leaving Christopher in the care of his nurses. They went home to their toddler Jason who needed them too. But when they stepped into their home, it felt strangely empty. When Jim went down the hall to tuck Jason in for the night, he glanced in the empty nursery. He went in and placed Christopher's little blue Bible in the empty crib.

As Sheila picked up the toys Jason had left around, she felt a pang of emptiness. When she looked at Christopher's empty infant chair, oh, how she missed the big, beautiful smile of her little butterball.

As she went to turn out the lights, she decided to leave on the light that shines over the picture of Jesus in their family room. The next morning Sheila awoke suddenly and remembered the empty crib down the hall. She thought of her baby in the hospital and ached to hold him.

The clock said, "4:30," but Sheila was unable to sleep. She went downstairs. Looking at her picture of Jesus, she prayed, "Lord, I need to feel You. I need to *feel* that You are real." In her mind He spoke to her. She saw Jesus in His soft, flowing robe, holding Christopher just as she wanted to hold him. Christopher seemed at home in His arms, just as he did in hers. Then she felt her Lord say, "Sheila, he's my baby too."

Sheila said to me later, "Dad, when Jesus said that, I didn't know if He meant that I was going to get to keep Christopher for a while longer, or if He was going to take Christopher to be with Him. But, it didn't matter. Either way, it didn't matter. For I had such peace. I felt my whole being bathed in peace because I had yielded my baby and my problems to Jesus. I knew that Jesus loved Christopher as much as I did, and that He was holding him for me even when I couldn't."

Yield your life and your problems to God. Let go and let God. A friend sent me this poem. I think it's terrific.

Let Go and Let God

As children bring their broken toys
    with tears for us to mend,

I brought my broken dreams to God,
    because He was my Friend.

But then, instead of leaving Him
    in peace to work alone,

I hung around and tried to help
    with ways that were my own.

At last I snatched them back and cried,
    "How can You be so slow?"

"My child," He said, "what could I do?
    You never did let go."

—UNKNOWN

Z Zip it up

Jesus said, "I am the Alpha and the Omega, the Beginning and the End, the First and the Last" (Rev. 22:13). If you live by this creed, x-ray your motives, and yield it all to God, then you come to the end and you can *zip it up*.

You can face whatever is ahead of you, and with Christ as your Friend, you can succeed.

Z_____

_____

_____

When the Queen of England visited Southern California, Mayor Tom Bradley invited a small group of celebrities to a private luncheon for Her Majesty and Prince Philip. I was honored to be included in that small group.

At the event a lady approached me whom I did not recognize. "You don't know me, Dr. Schuller," she said, continuing, "but I'm John Wayne's daughter. I know that you and Dad were good friends. I know that you prayed for him before his surgery in Newport Beach. But I don't know if anybody told you about what happened in his life before he died." She smiled, her eyes glazed in a mist of love.

"He never missed your telecast. One Sunday morning you did something you very seldom have done. You said, 'There must come the time in our life when we really surrender our life entirely to the Lord. Today may be the day when you should slip out of the chair, get down on your knees, and yield your life completely to God. Ask Him to forgive you of your sins. Ask Him to save your immortal soul.'"

Now as she looked at me, John Wayne's daughter said, "Dr. Schuller, my father was so sick in his bed—but he got out of his bed, got down on his knees, and prayed your closing prayer with you and turned his life completely over to the Lord!"

Probably no person has an image for being a tougher tough guy than John Wayne. Yet, even he found that to face the ultimate battle he needed superstrength. And that's what God provides when we turn our lives over completely to Him.

"If God is for us, who can be against us?" (Rom. 8:31) That is the ultimate secret of becoming tough enough to face the toughest battle and win! Only then can you be sure that your life will prove the truth of the title of this book: "Tough times never last, but tough people do!"—eternally!

It is my prayer that this book has been an answer to the most important prayer that you could be praying today:

Lord,
give me
the guidance
to know
when to hold on
and
when to let go
and the grace
to make
the right decision
with dignity.

About the Author

ROBERT H. SCHULLER is founder and senior minister
of the famed Crystal Cathedral in Garden Grove,
California. His telecast, *The Hour of Power*, is one
of the most widely viewed programs in television
history. The author of fifteen books, Dr. Schuller
has received numerous awards as well as several
honorary degrees. His latest book, *Stealing From
Our Children*, has recently been published in
paperback by Bantam.

HEARTWARMING BOOKS
OF
FAITH AND INSPIRATION